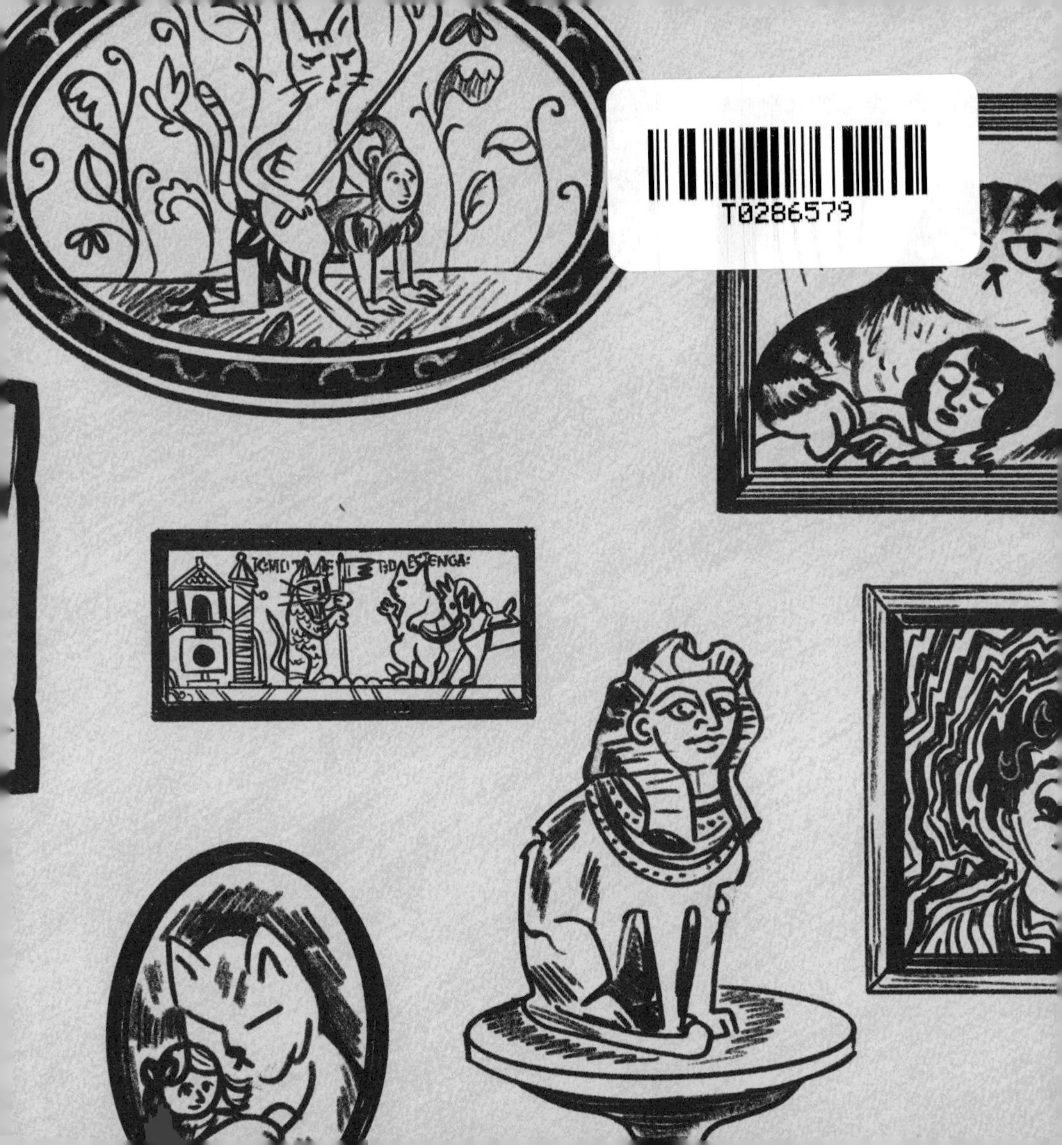

CAT PEOPLE

A Comic Collection

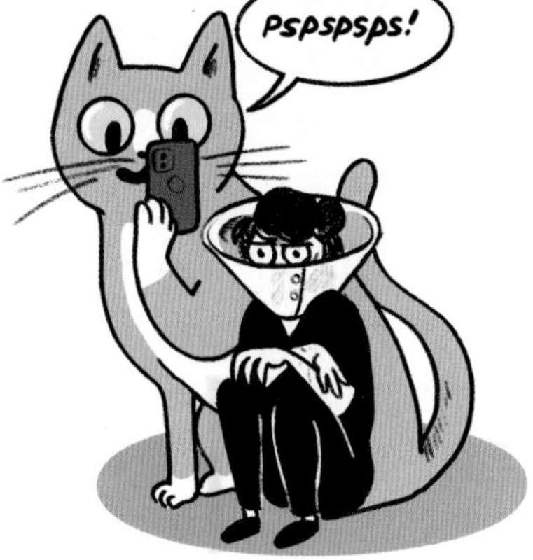
PSPSPSPS!

HANNAH HILLAM

RUNNING PRESS
PHILADELPHIA

Running Press
Hachette Book Group
1290 Avenue of the Americas, New York, NY 10104
www.runningpress.com
@Running_Press

First Edition: October 2024

Published by Running Press, an imprint of Hachette Book Group, Inc. The Running Press name and logo are trademarks of Hachette Book Group, Inc.

The Hachette Speakers Bureau provides a wide range of authors for speaking events. To find out more, go to www.hachettespeakersbureau.com or email HachetteSpeakers@hbgusa.com.

Running Press books may be purchased in bulk for business, educational, or promotional use. For more information, please contact your local bookseller or the Hachette Book Group Special Markets Department at Special.Markets@hbgusa.com.

The publisher is not responsible for websites (or their content) that are not owned by the publisher.

Print book cover design by Jenna McBride
Interior design by Clea Chmela

Library of Congress Control Number: 2024932529

ISBNs: 978-0-7624-8608-3 (hardcover), 978-0-7624-8609-0 (ebook)

Printed in China

APS

10 9 8 7 6 5 4 3 2 1

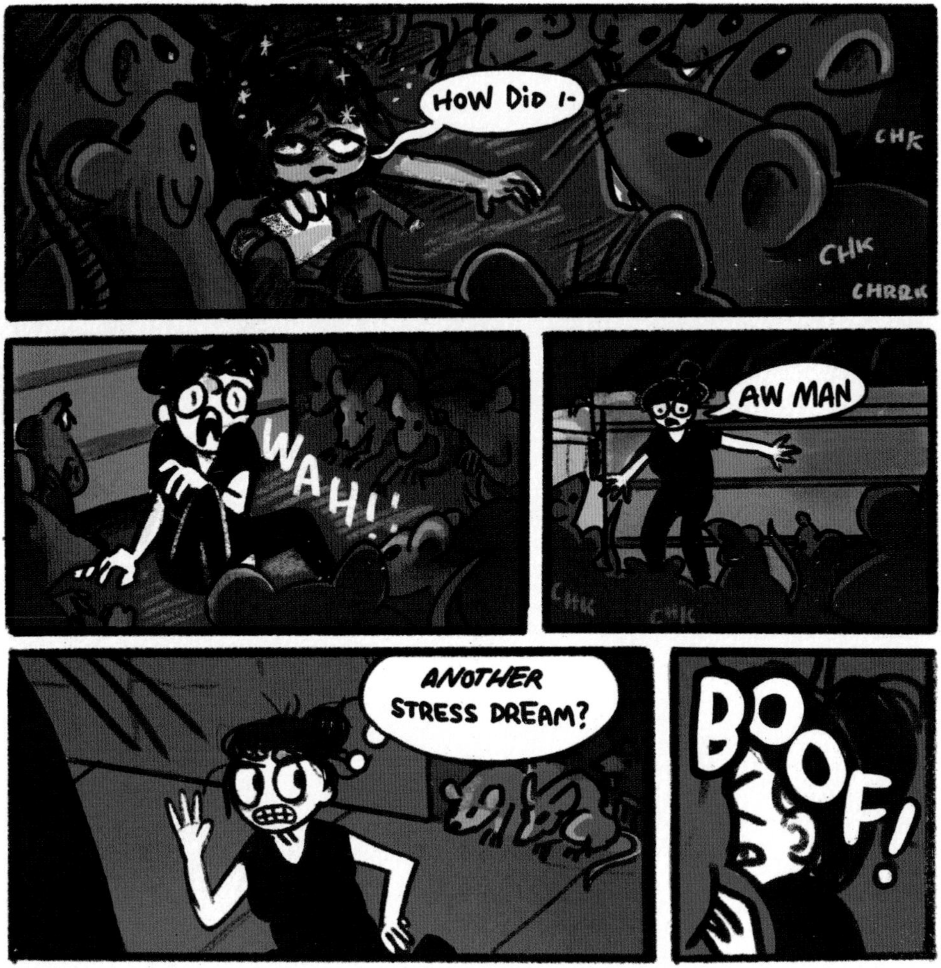
HOW DID I-
CHK
CHK
CHRRK
WAH!!
AW MAN
CHK
CHK
ANOTHER STRESS DREAM?
BOOF!

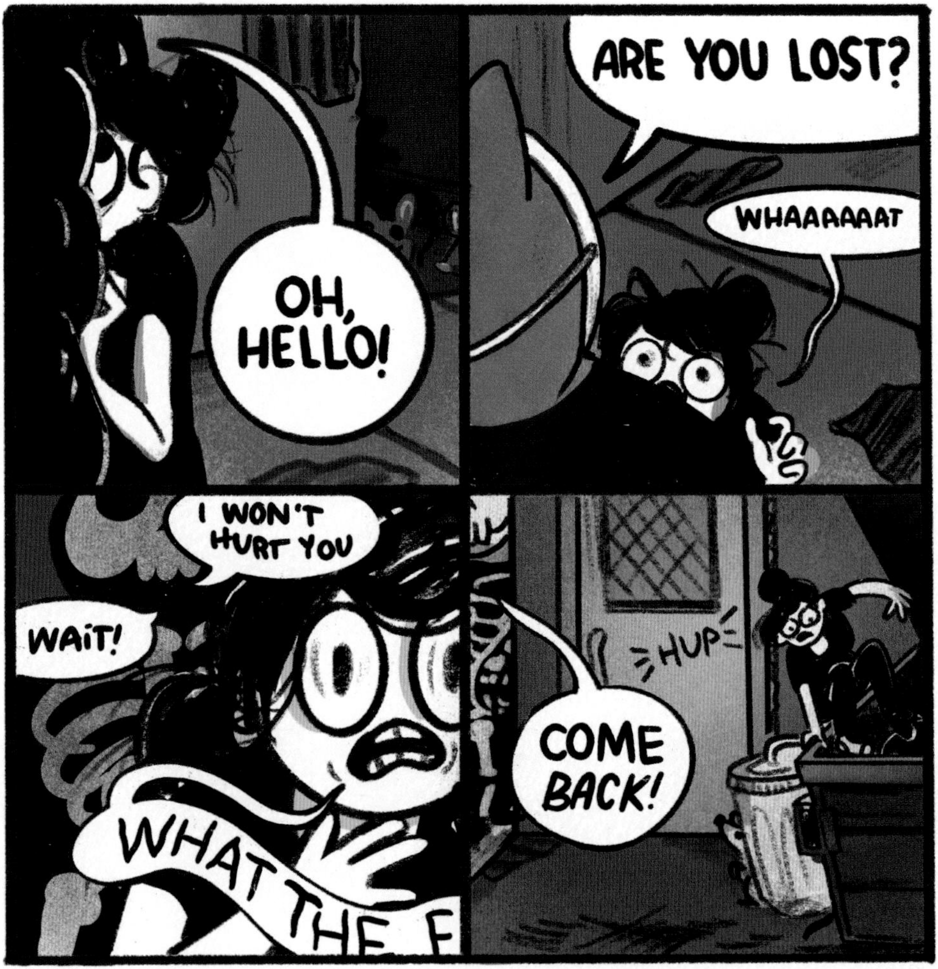
OH, HELLO!
ARE YOU LOST?
WHAAAAAAT
I WON'T HURT YOU
WAIT!
WHAT THE F
HUP
COME BACK!

For Sean and his favorite cat, Mouse

"Look into the eyes of a cat for a moment. Your gaze will flicker between recognising another being (without quite being able to situate it), and staring into a void."

—DAVID WOOD, "IF A CAT COULD TALK," *AEON*

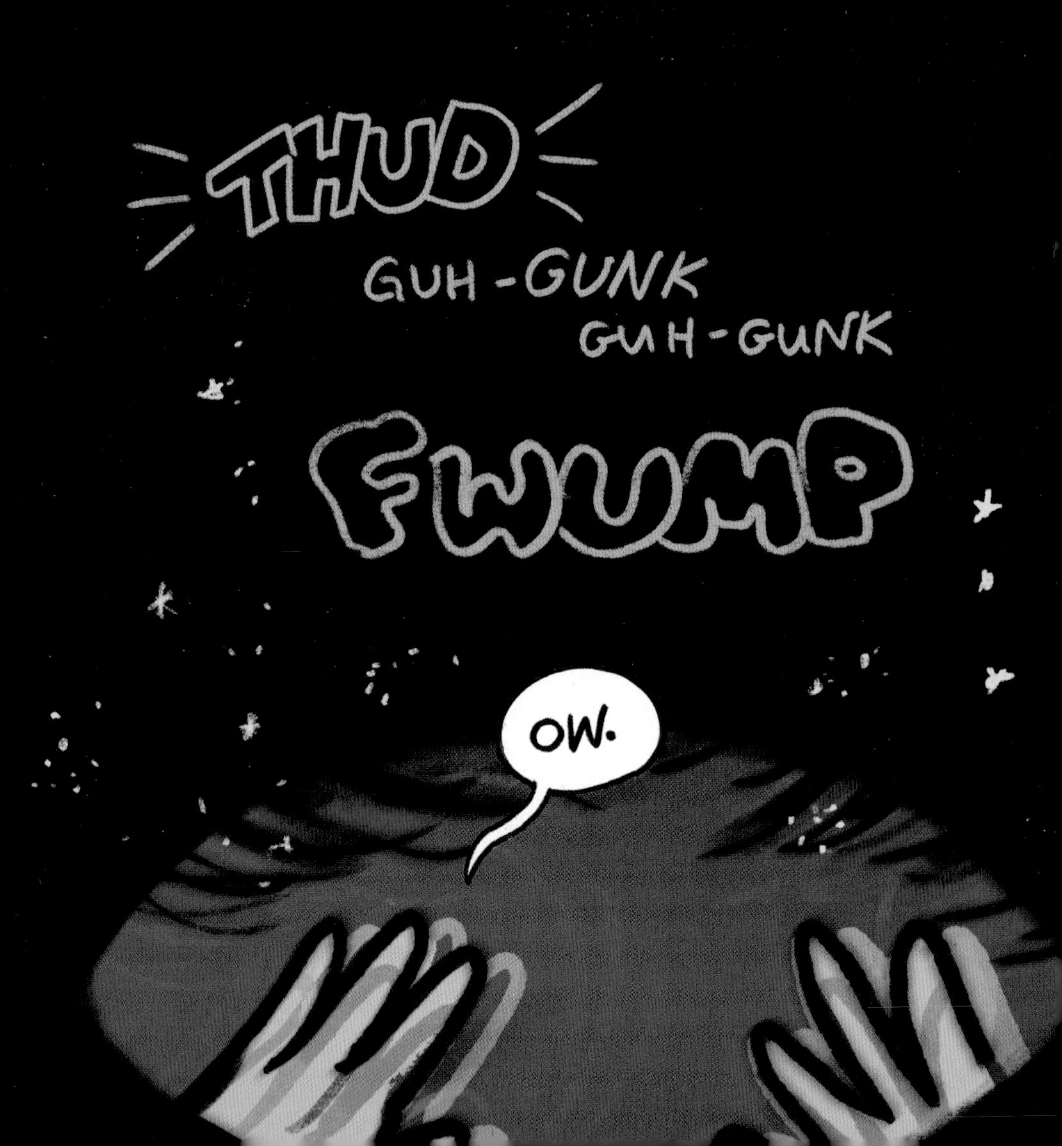
THUD
GUH-GUNK
GUH-GUNK
FWUMP
OW.

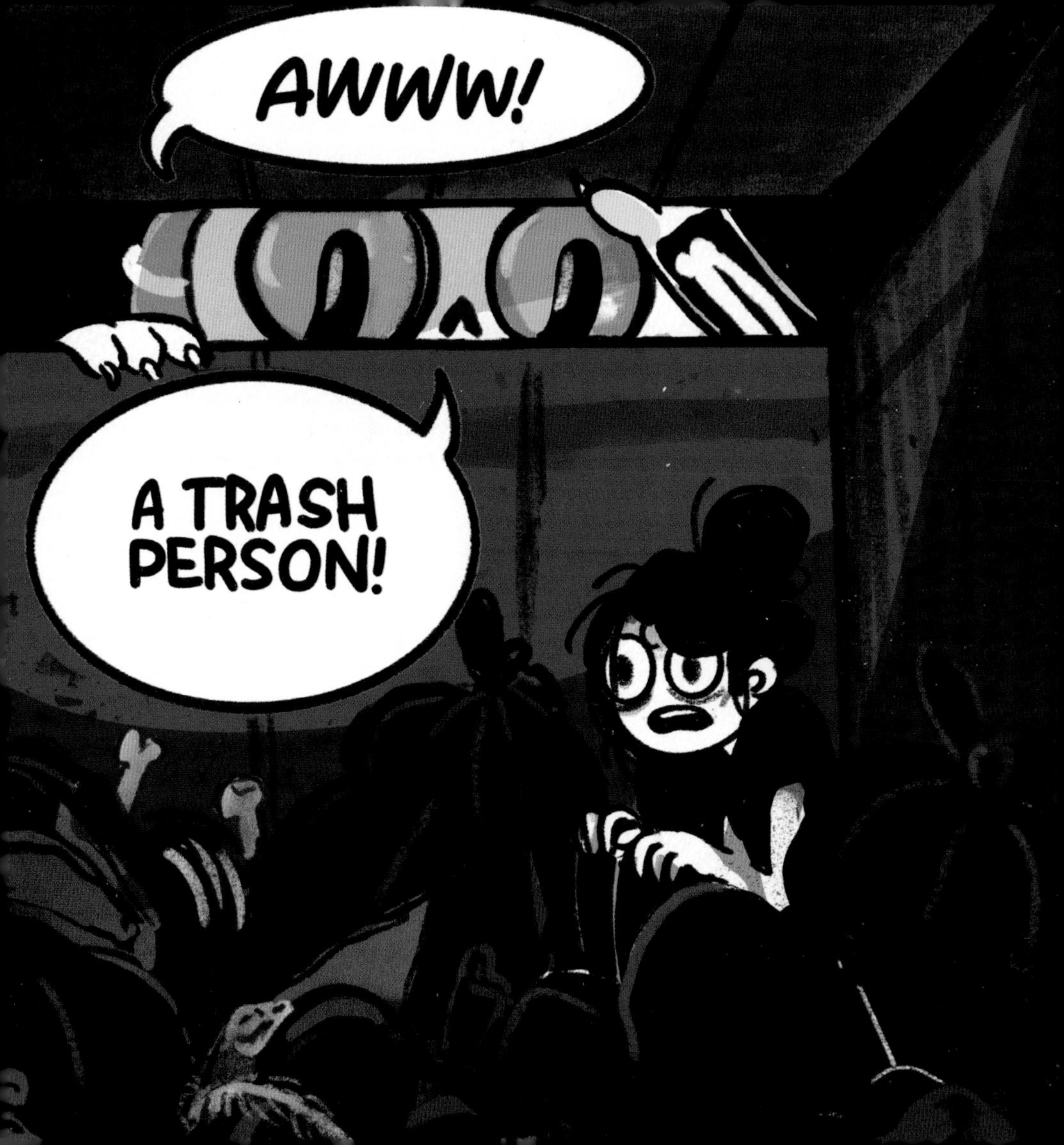
AWWW!
A TRASH PERSON!

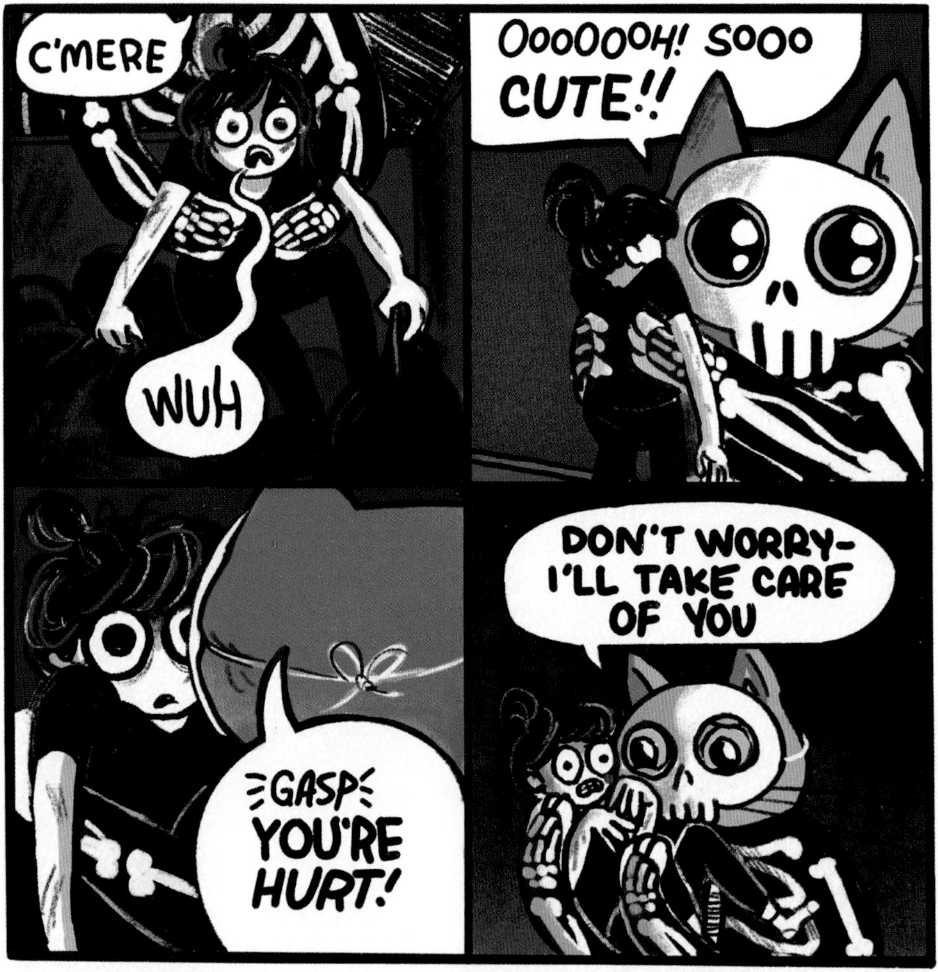
C'MERE
WUH
OOOOOOH! SOOO CUTE!!
GASP YOU'RE HURT!
DON'T WORRY- I'LL TAKE CARE OF YOU

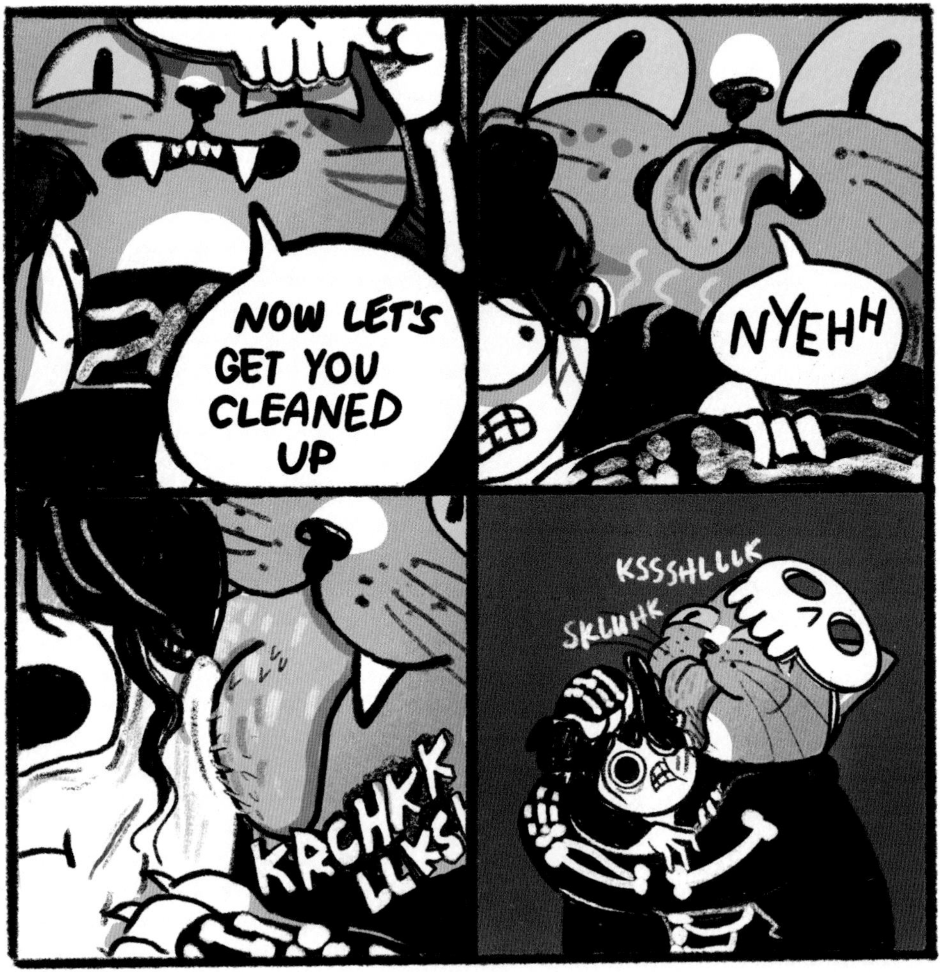
NOW LET'S GET YOU CLEANED UP
NYEHH
KRCHKK LLKS!
KSSSHLLLK
SKLUHK

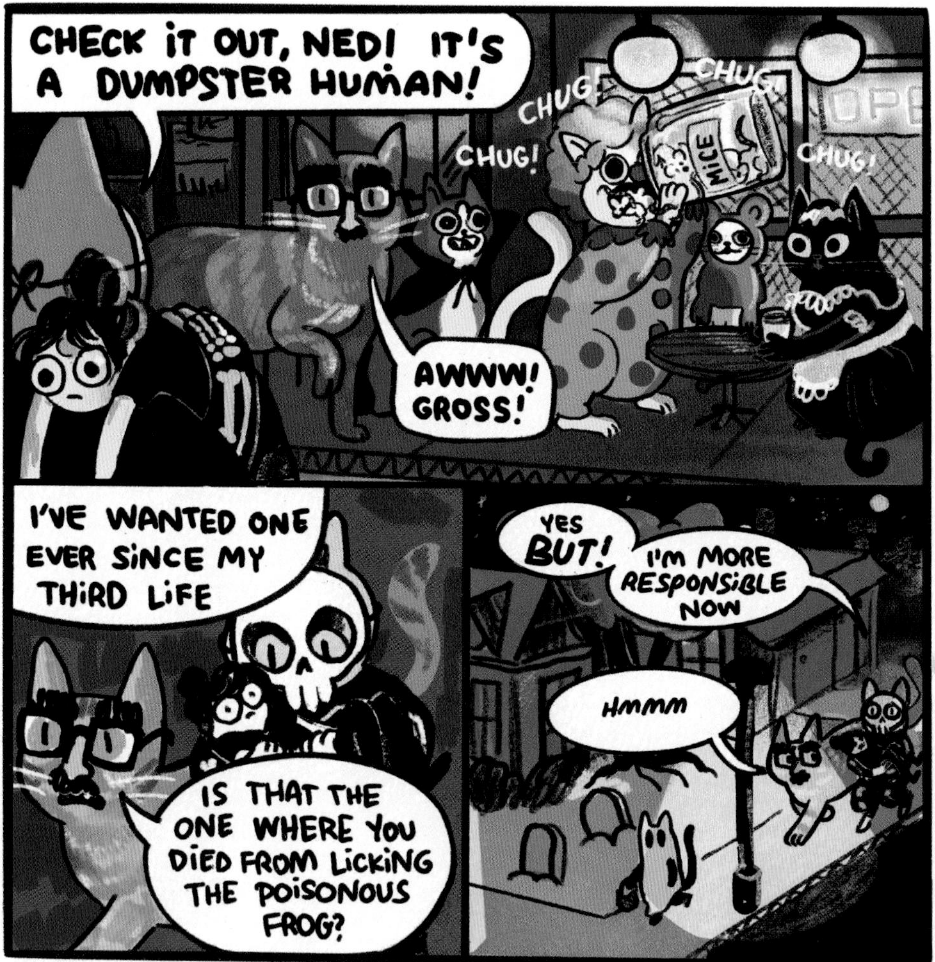
CHECK iT OUT, NED! IT'S A DUMPSTER HUMAN!
CHUG! CHUG! CHUG! CHUG! CHUG!
MiCE
AWWW! GROSS!
I'VE WANTED ONE EVER SiNCE MY THiRD LiFE
IS THAT THE ONE WHERE YOU DIED FROM LICKING THE POISONOUS FROG?
YES BUT!
I'M MORE RESPONSIBLE NOW
HMMM

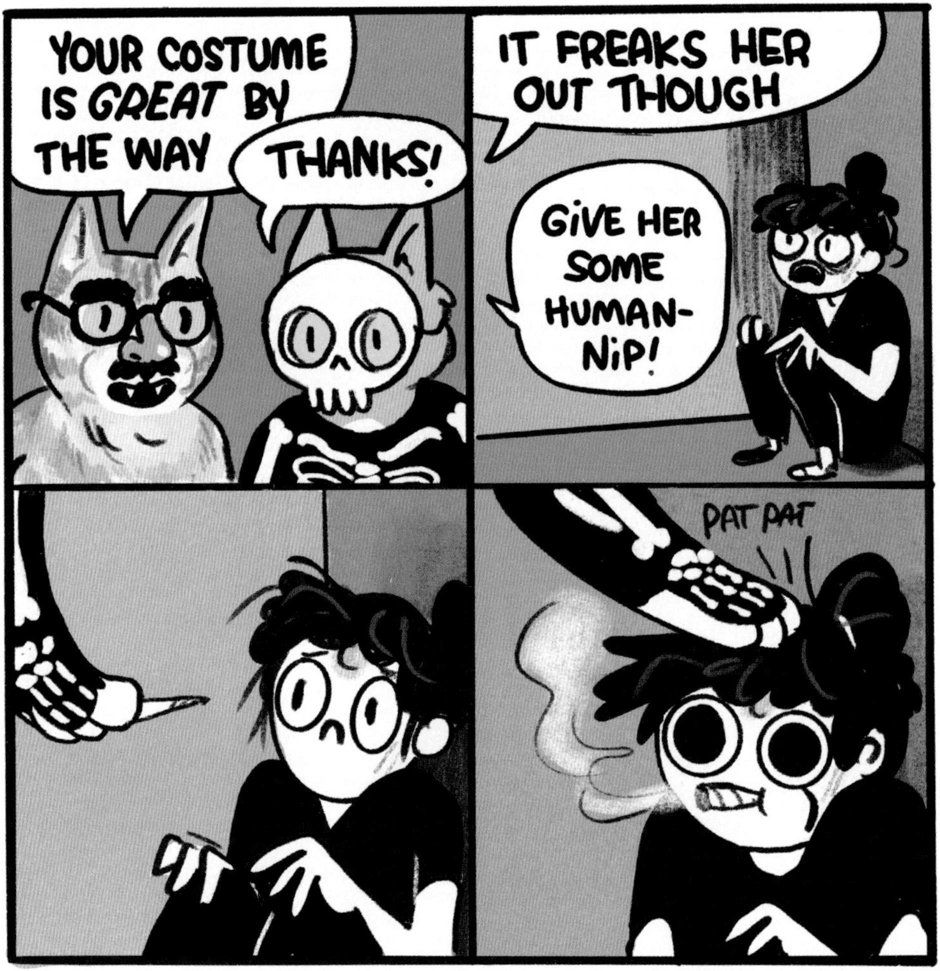
YOUR COSTUME IS *GREAT* BY THE WAY
THANKS!
IT FREAKS HER OUT THOUGH
GIVE HER SOME HUMAN-NIP!
PAT PAT

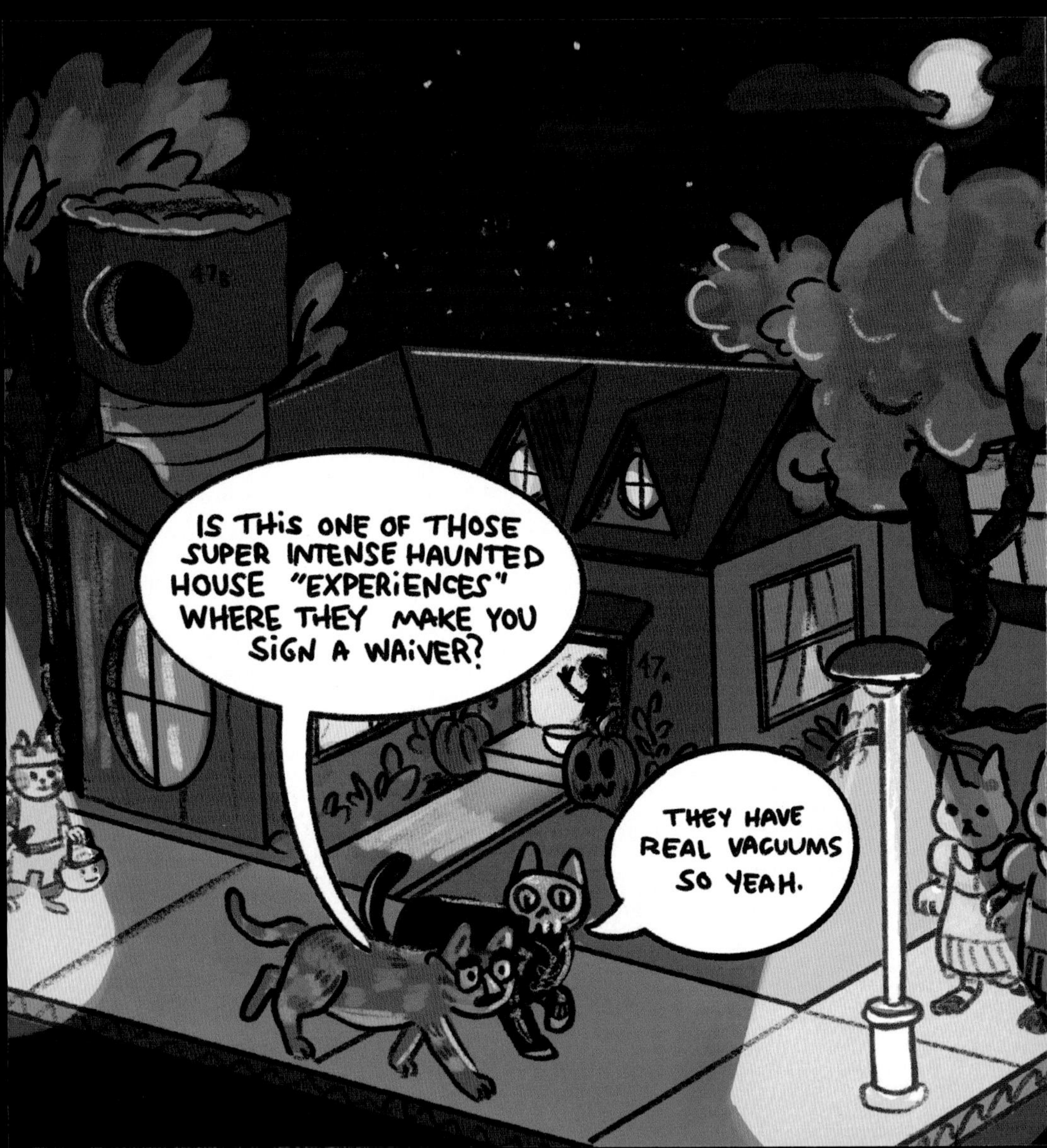
IS THIS ONE OF THOSE SUPER INTENSE HAUNTED HOUSE "EXPERIENCES" WHERE THEY MAKE YOU SIGN A WAIVER?
THEY HAVE REAL VACUUMS SO YEAH.

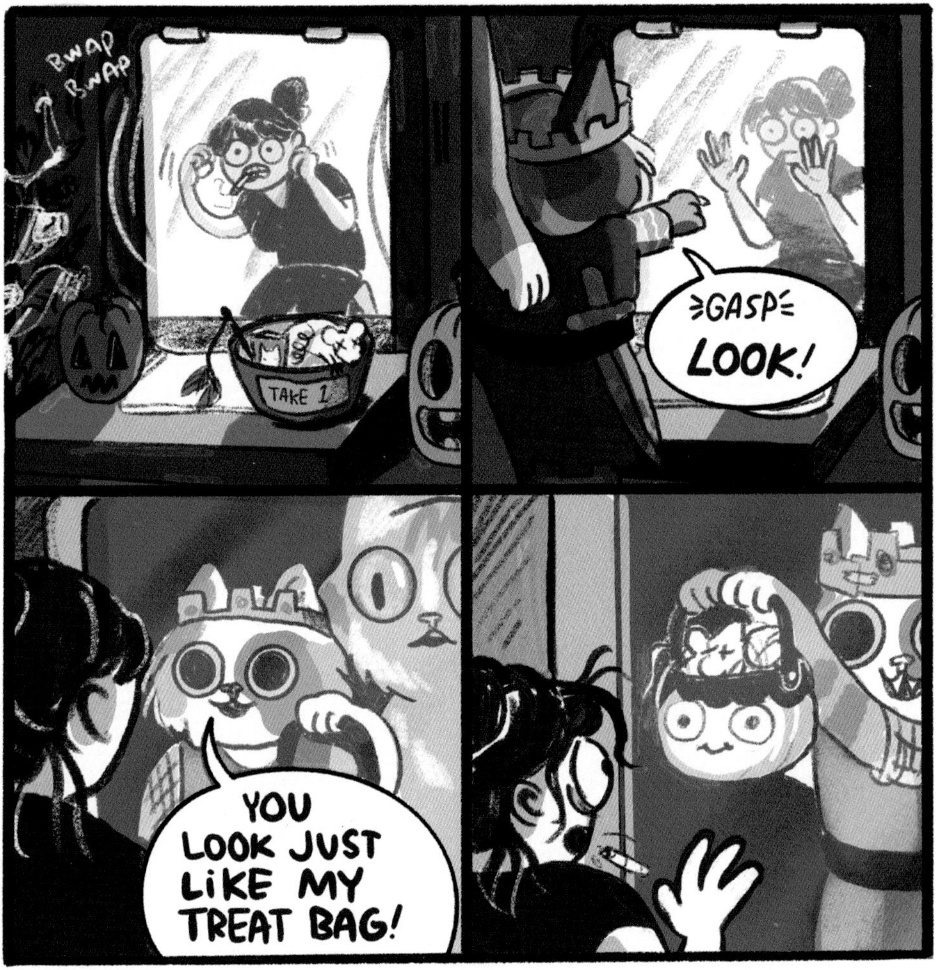
BWAP
BWAP
TAKE 1
GASP
LOOK!
YOU
LOOK JUST
LIKE MY
TREAT BAG!

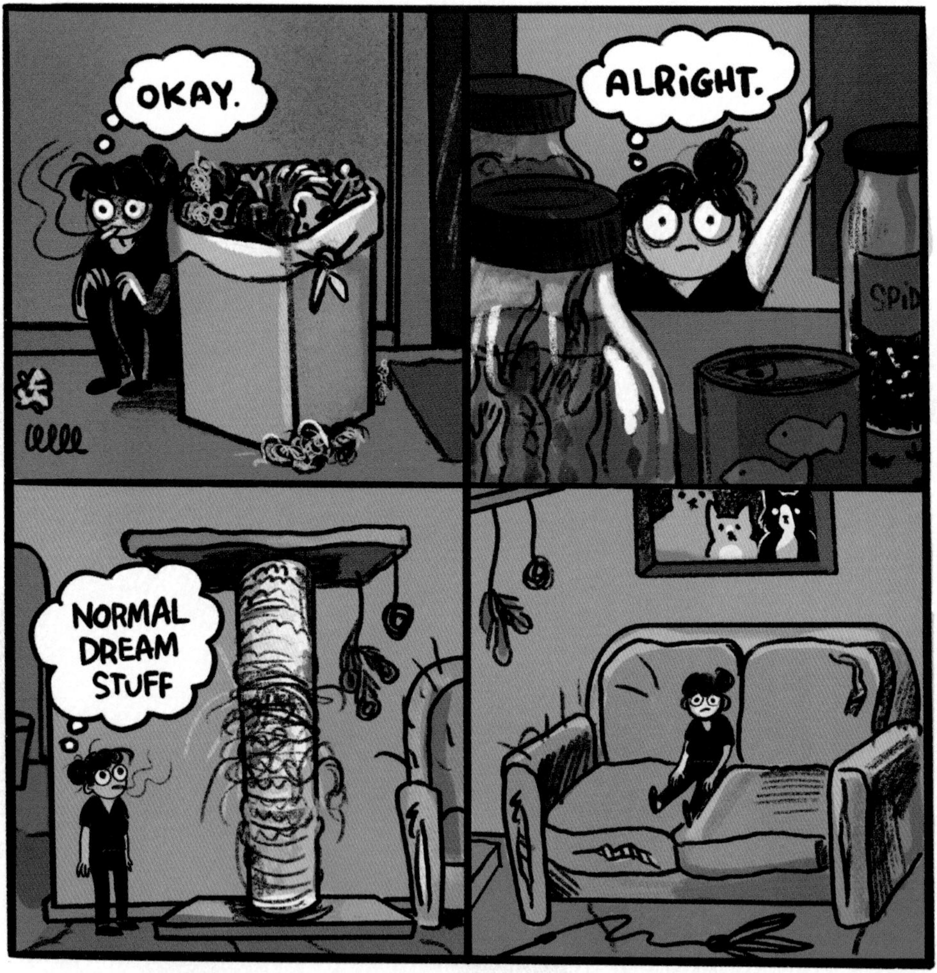
OKAY.
ALRIGHT.
SPI
NORMAL DREAM STUFF

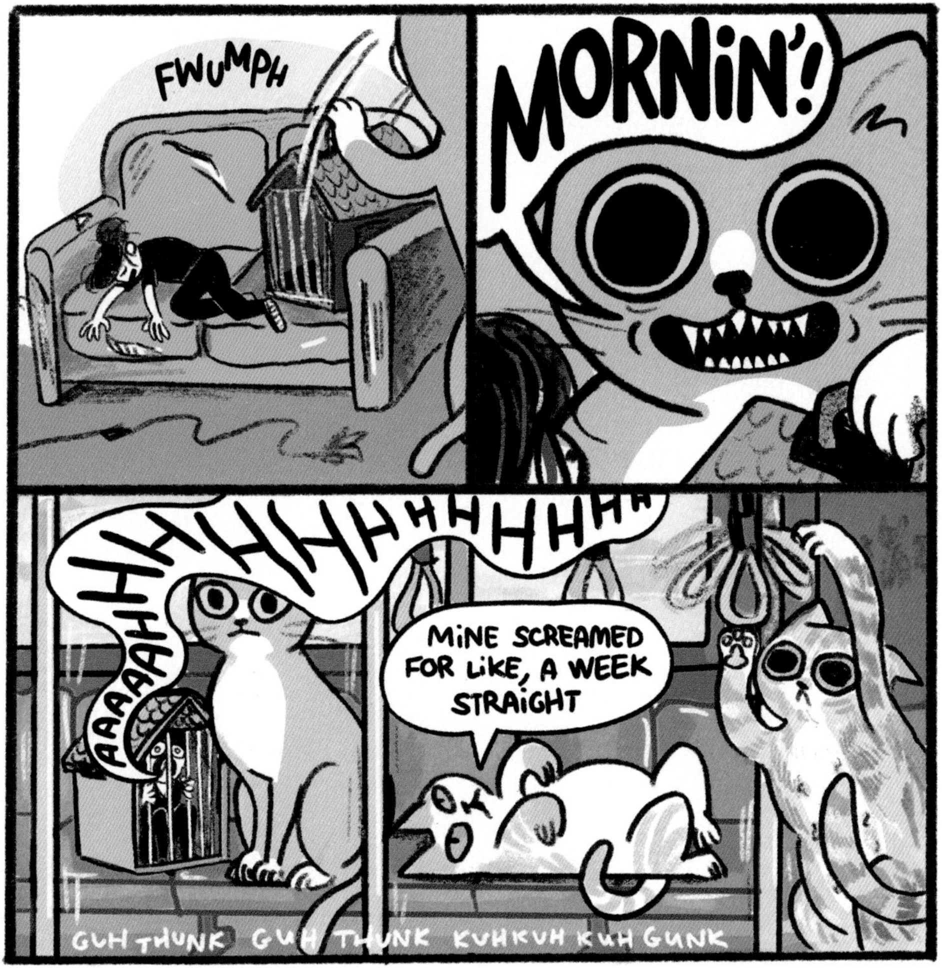
FWUMPH
MORNIN'!
AAAAAAHHHHHHHHHHHHHH
MINE SCREAMED FOR LIKE, A WEEK STRAIGHT
GUH THUNK GUH THUNK KUHKUH KUH GUNK

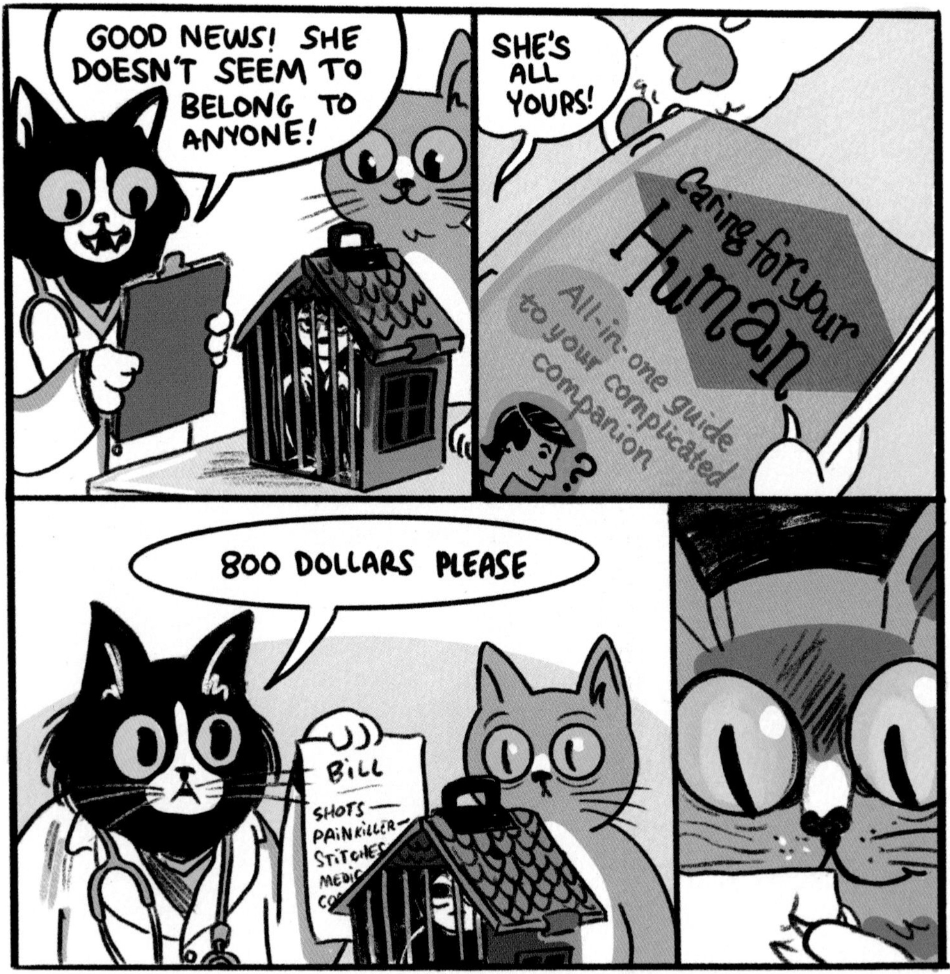
GOOD NEWS! SHE DOESN'T SEEM TO BELONG TO ANYONE!
SHE'S ALL YOURS!
Caring for your Human
All-in-one guide to your complicated companion
?
800 DOLLARS PLEASE
BILL
SHOTS
PAINKILLER

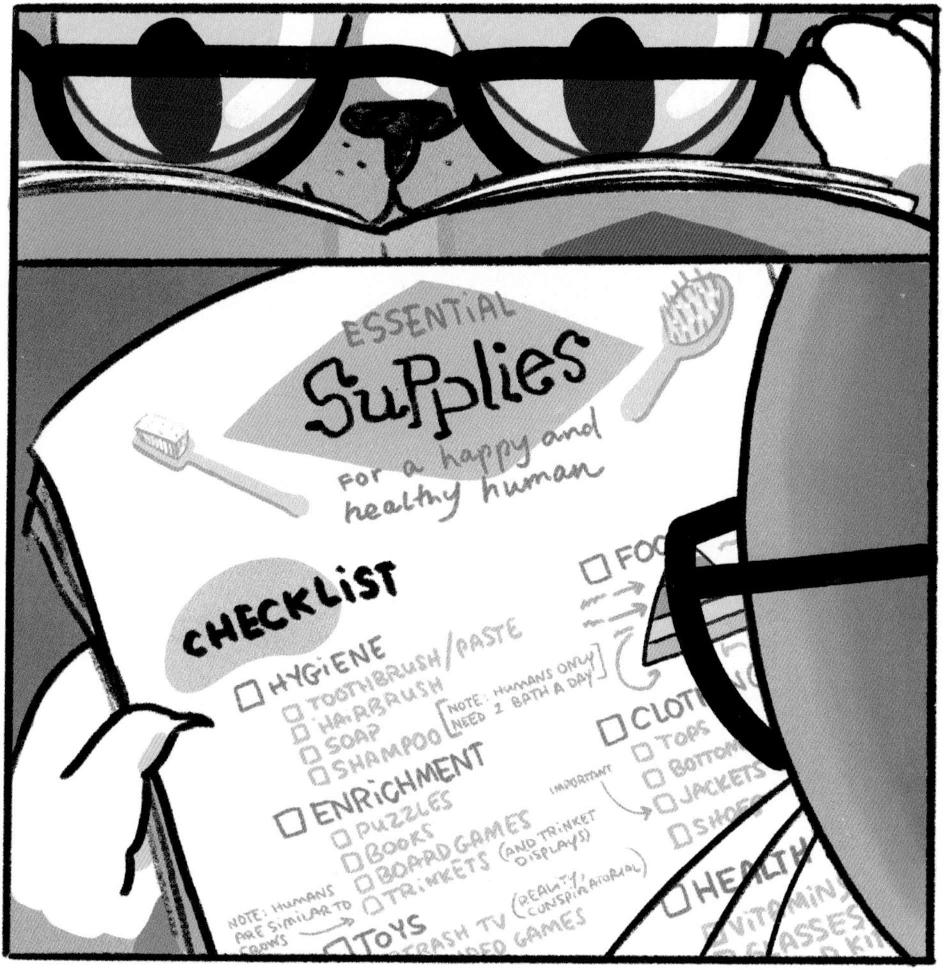
ESSENTIAL
Supplies
for a happy and healthy human
CHECKLIST
HYGIENE
TOOTHBRUSH/PASTE
HAIRBRUSH
SOAP
SHAMPOO
NOTE: HUMANS ONLY NEED 1 BATH A DAY
ENRICHMENT
PUZZLES
BOOKS
BOARD GAMES
TRINKETS (AND TRINKET DISPLAYS)
TRASH TV (REALITY/CONSPIRATORIAL)
NOTE: HUMANS ARE SIMILAR TO CROWS
TOYS
IMPORTANT
TOPS
JACKETS
HEALTH

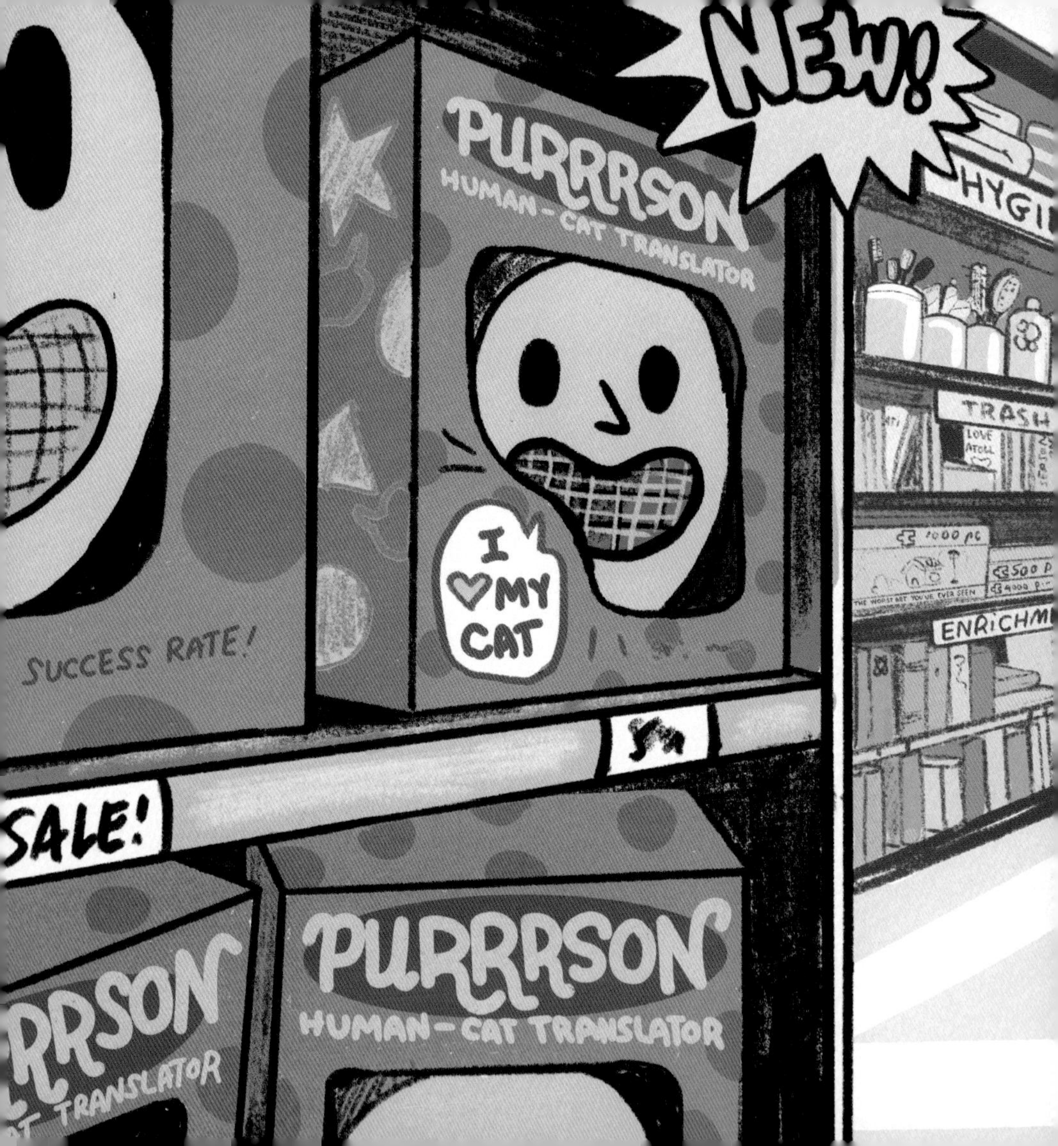
NEW!
PURRRSON
HUMAN-CAT TRANSLATOR
I ♥ MY CAT
SUCCESS RATE!
HYGI
TRASH
ENRICHM
SALE!
PURRRSON
HUMAN-CAT TRANSLATOR
RRSON
TRANSLATOR

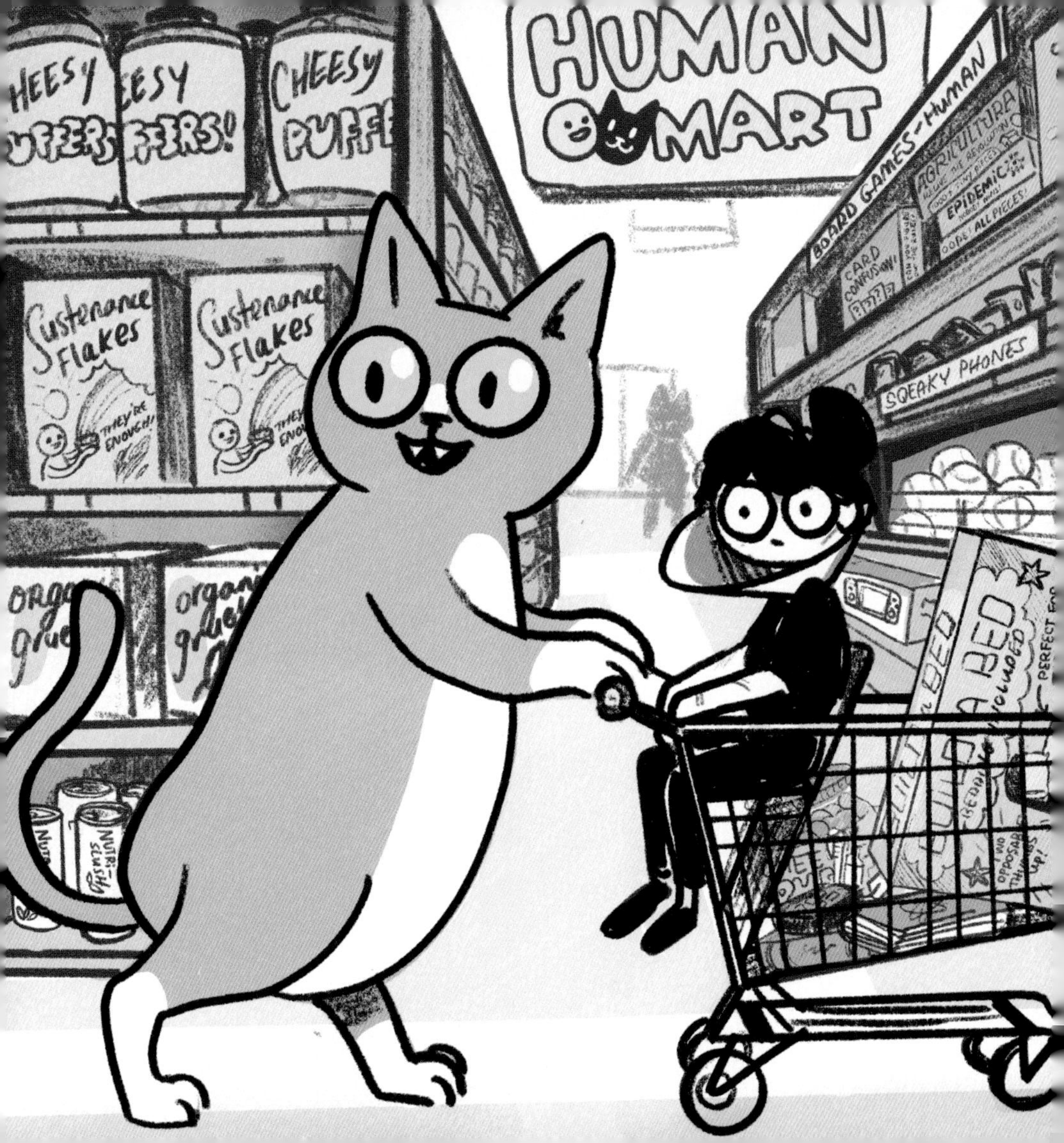
HUMAN MART
CHEESy
CHEESy
Sustenance Flakes
THEY'RE ENOUGH!
Sustenance Flakes
BOARD GAMES-HUMAN
AGRICULTURA
EPIDEMIC
OOPS! ALL PIECES!
CARD CONFUSION!
SQEAKY PHONES
NUTRI-SLUSH
A BED
PERFECT FOR

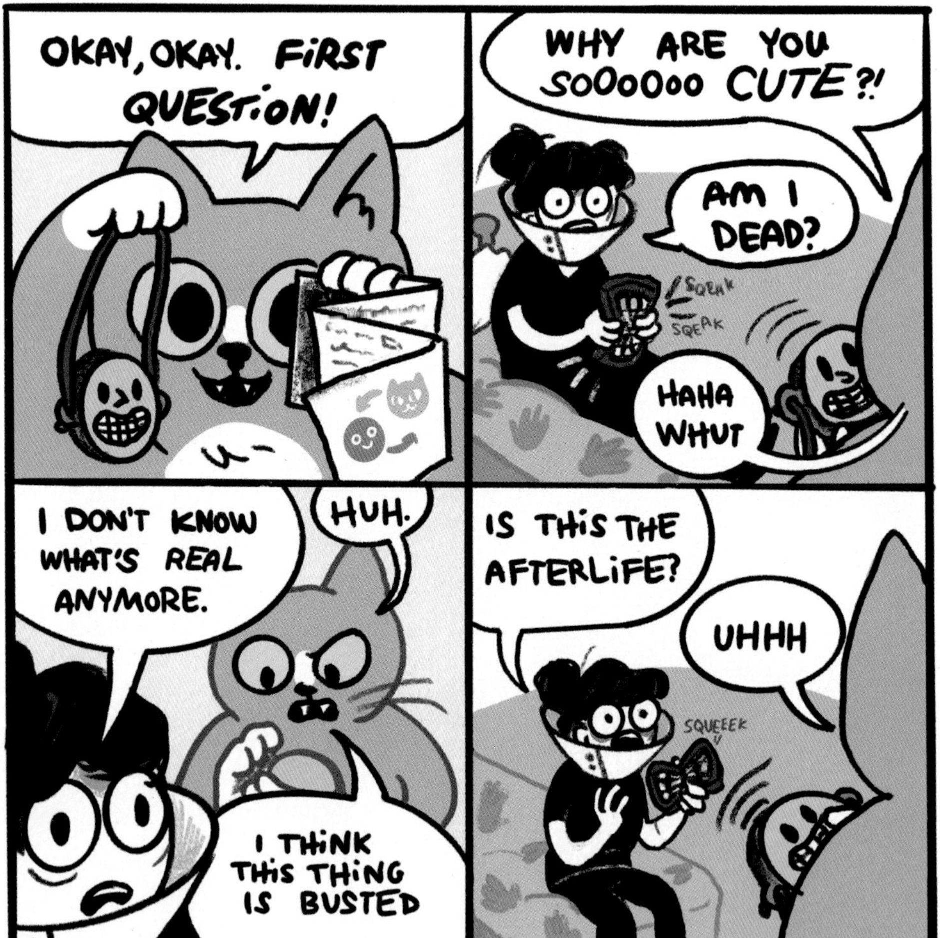

OKAY, OKAY. FIRST QUESTION!
WHY ARE YOU SOOoOoo CUTE?!
AM I DEAD?
SQEAK
SQEAK
HAHA WHUT
I DON'T KNOW WHAT'S REAL ANYMORE.
HUH.
I THINK THIS THING IS BUSTED
IS THIS THE AFTERLIFE?
UHHH
SQUEEEK

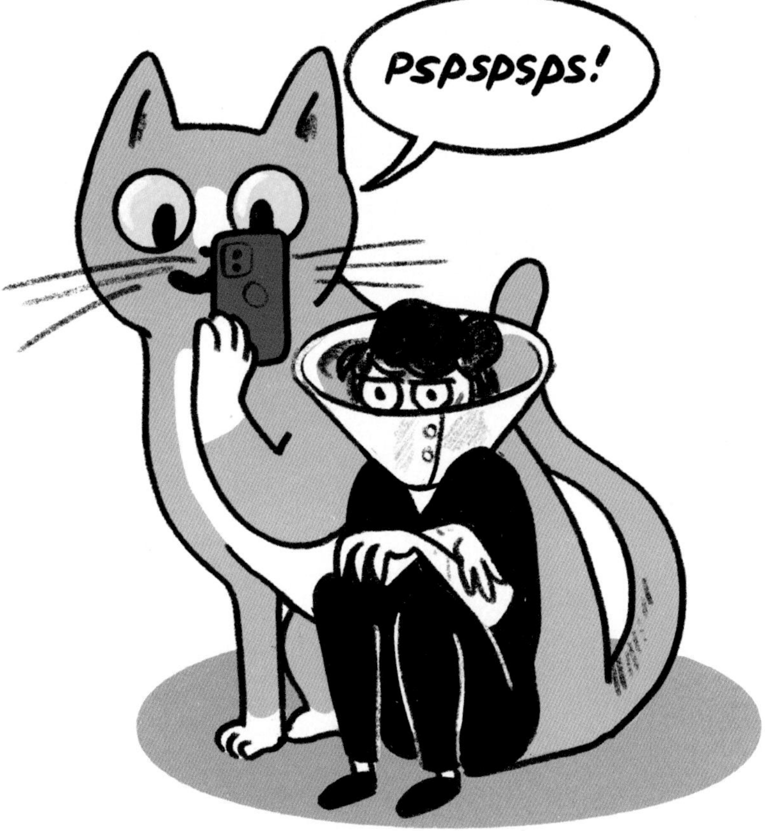
PSPSPSPS!

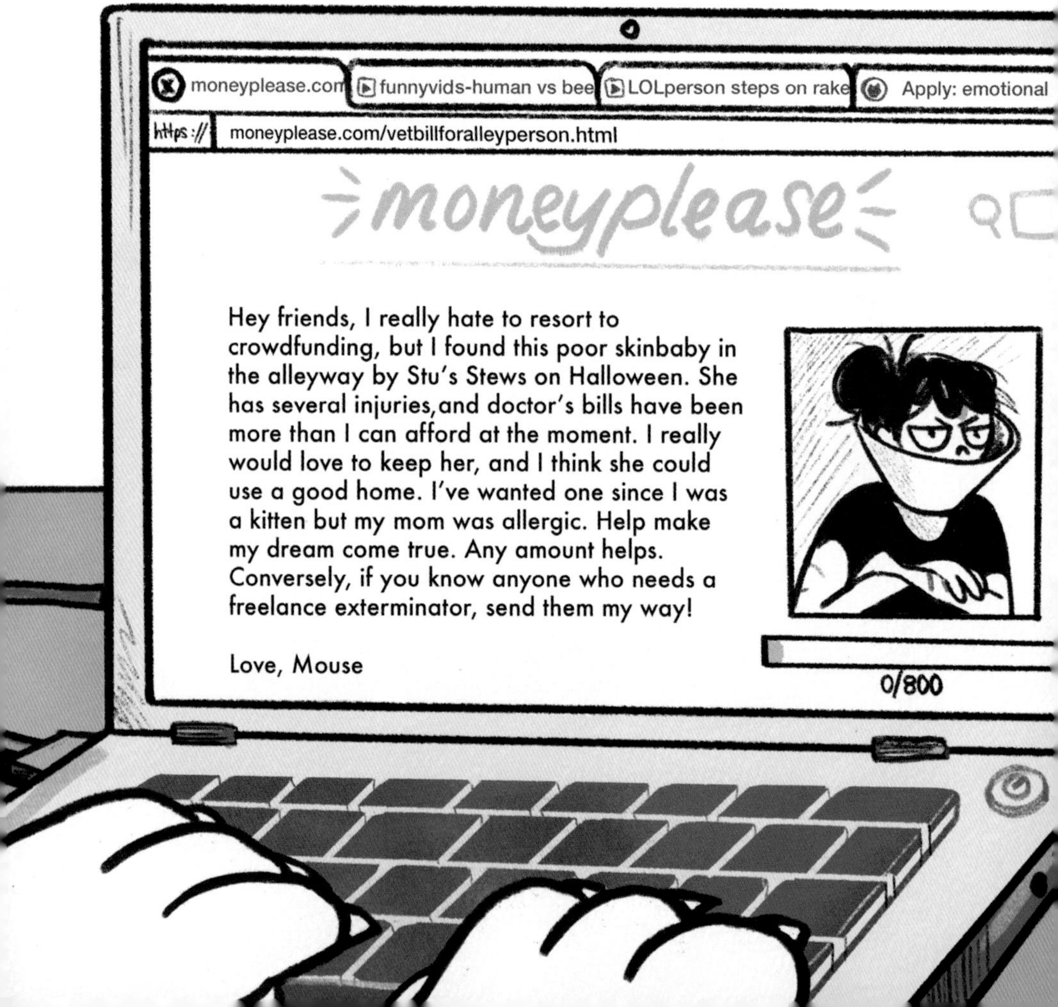

moneyplease.com
funnyvids-human vs bee
LOLperson steps on rake
Apply: emotional
https://
moneyplease.com/vetbillforalleyperson.html
moneyplease
Hey friends, I really hate to resort to crowdfunding, but I found this poor skinbaby in the alleyway by Stu's Stews on Halloween. She has several injuries, and doctor's bills have been more than I can afford at the moment. I really would love to keep her, and I think she could use a good home. I've wanted one since I was a kitten but my mom was allergic. Help make my dream come true. Any amount helps. Conversely, if you know anyone who needs a freelance exterminator, send them my way!
Love, Mouse
0/800

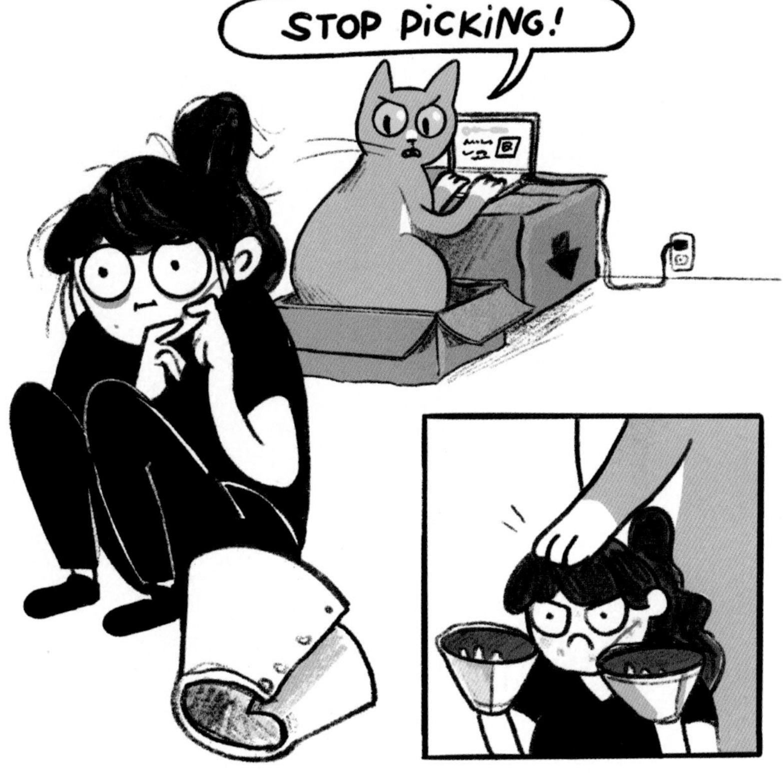
STOP PICKING!

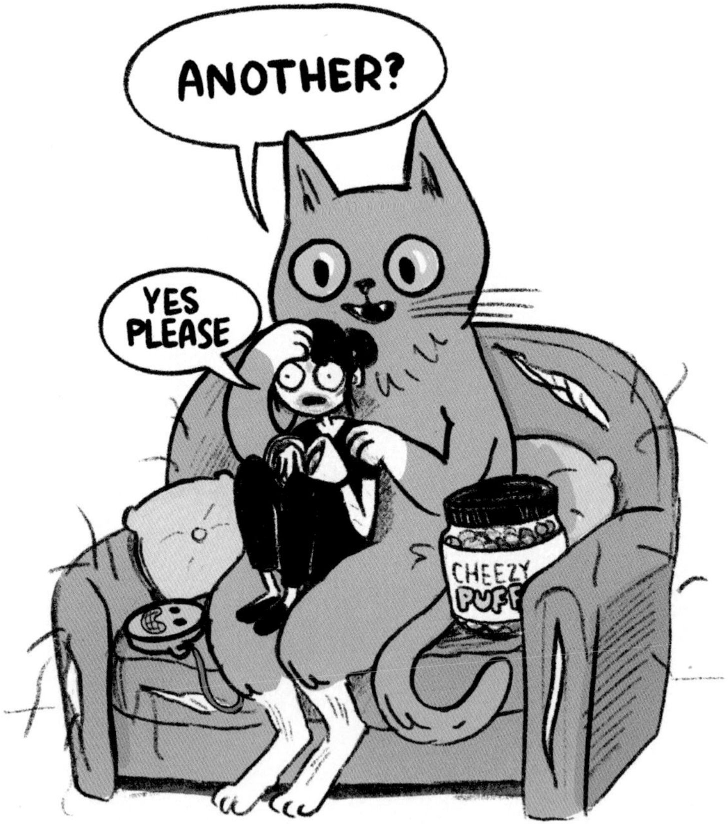
ANOTHER?
YES PLEASE
CHEEZY PUFF

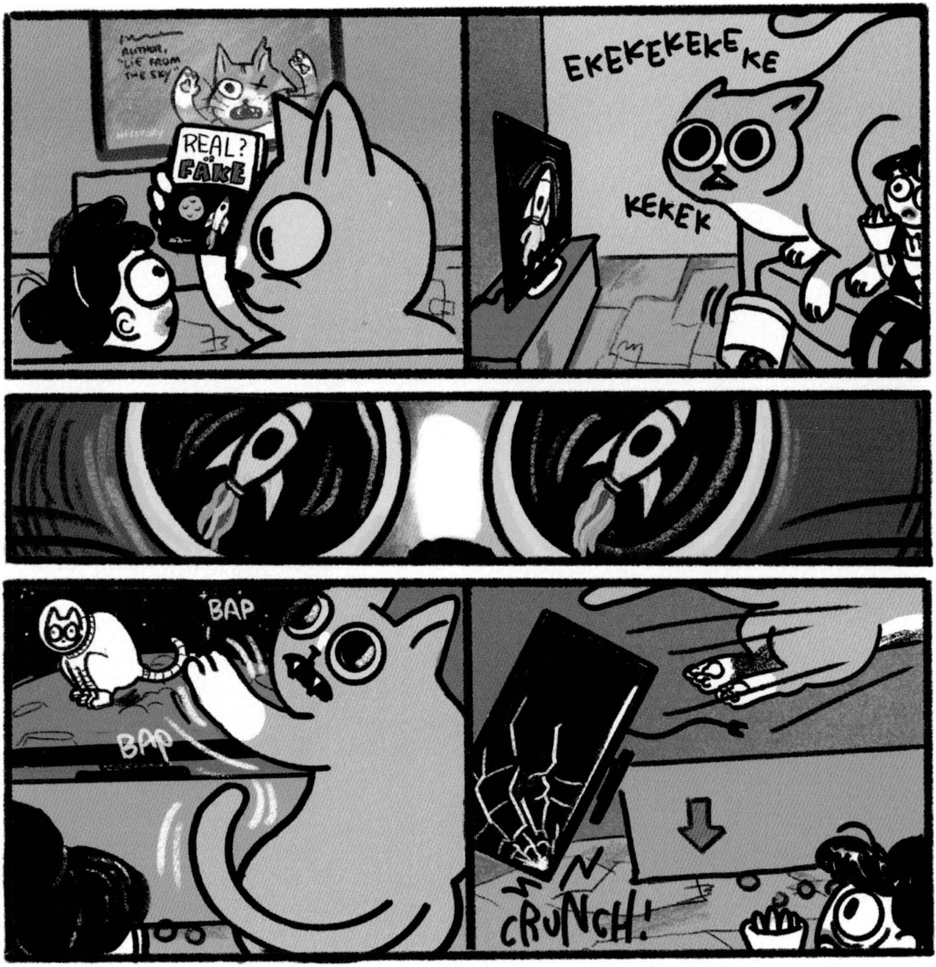
AUTHOR,
"LIE FROM
THE SKY"
REAL?
OR
FAKE
EKEKEKEKEKE KE
KEKEK
BAP
BAP
CRUNCH!

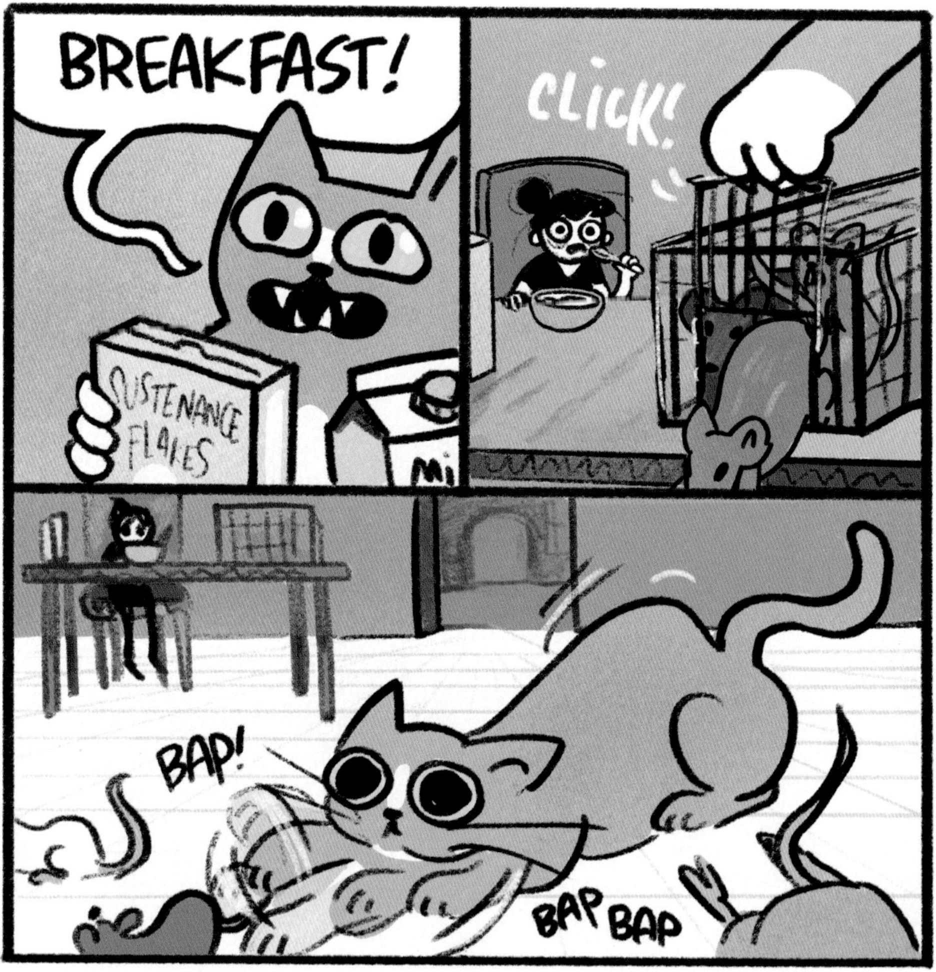
BREAKFAST!
SUSTENANCE FLAKES
Mi
CLICK!
BAP!
BAP BAP

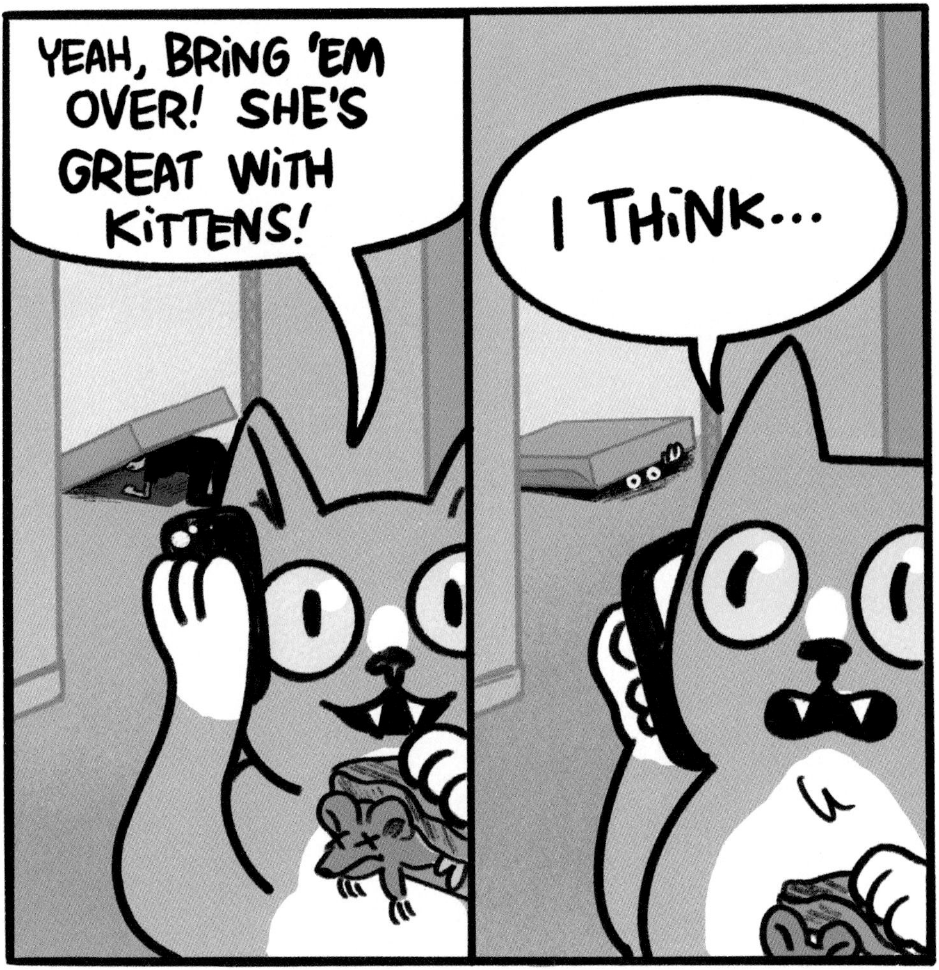
YEAH, BRING 'EM OVER! SHE'S GREAT WITH KITTENS!
I THINK...

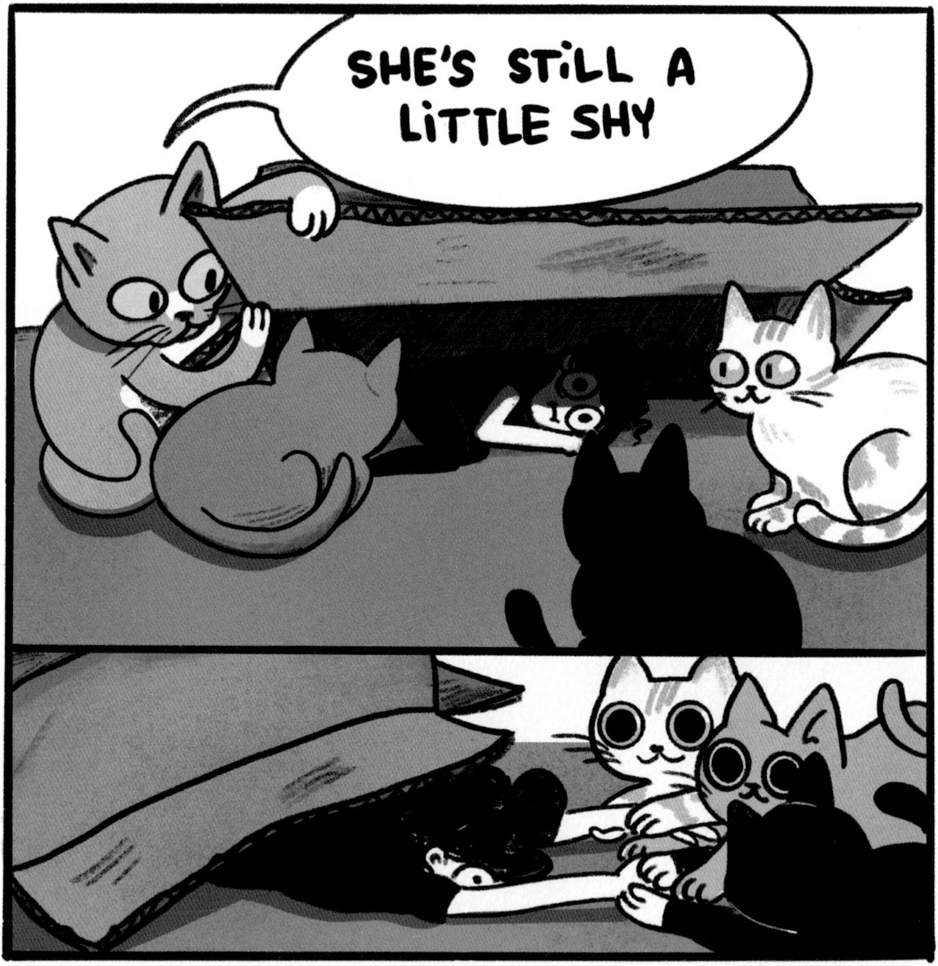
SHE'S STiLL A LiTTLE SHY

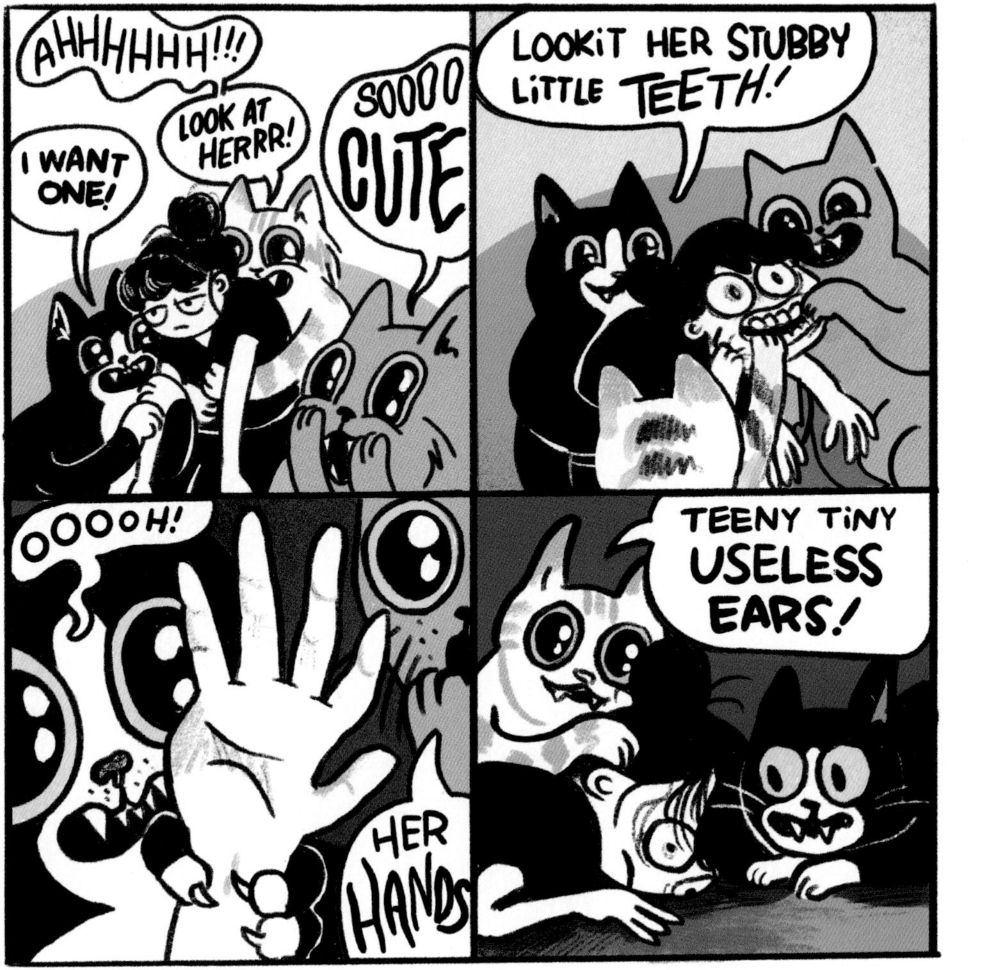
AHHHHHH!!!
I WANT ONE!
LOOK AT HERRR!
SOOOO CUTE
LOOKiT HER STUBBY LiTTLE TEETH!
OOOOH!
HER HANDS
TEENY TiNY USELESS EARS!

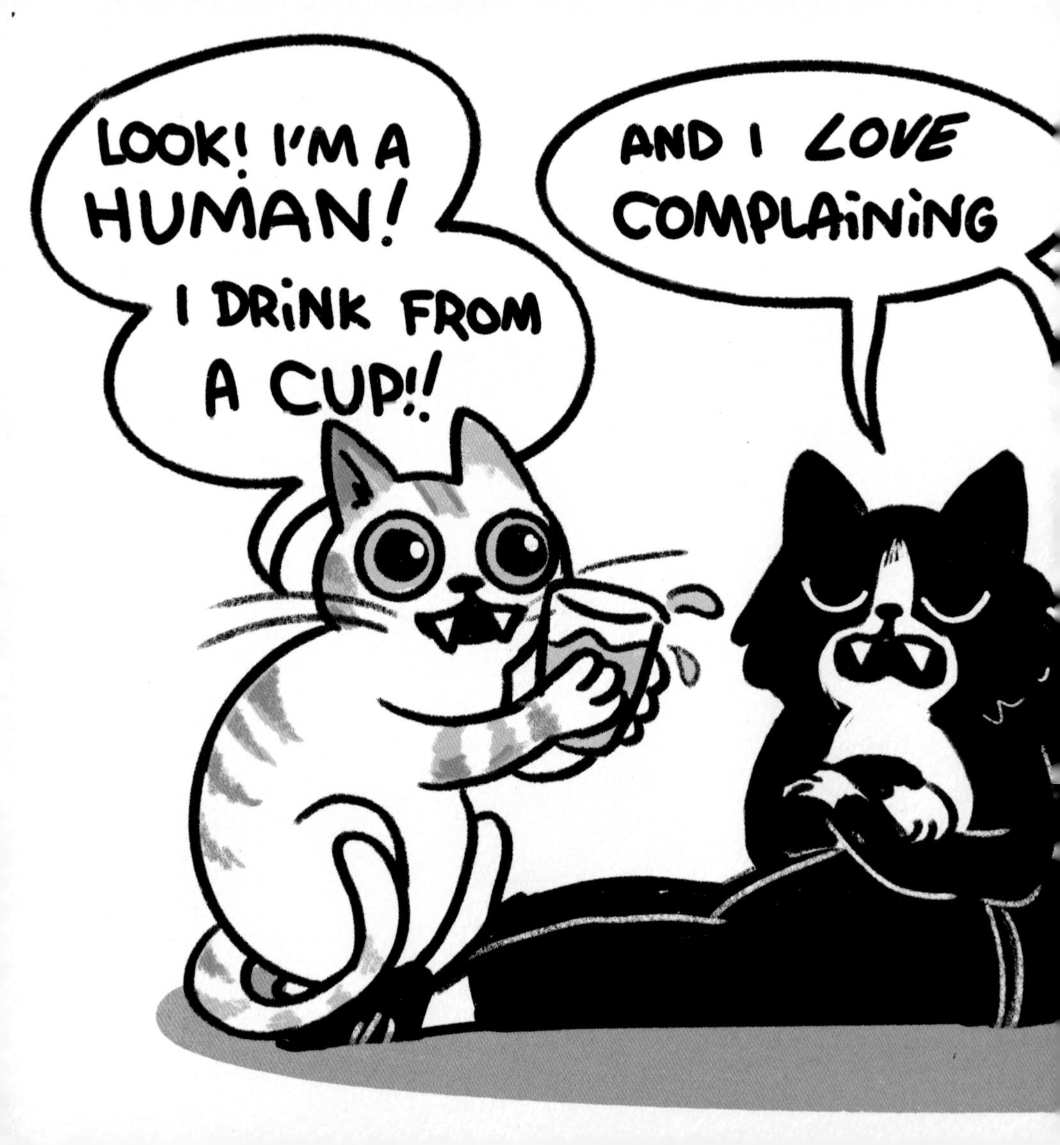
LOOK! I'M A HUMAN!
I DRINK FROM A CUP!!
AND I LOVE COMPLAINING

UH OH! I'M GONNA PUKE IN THE TOILET INSTEAD OF ALL OVER THE FLOOOR
I'M SO TIRED ALL THE TIME

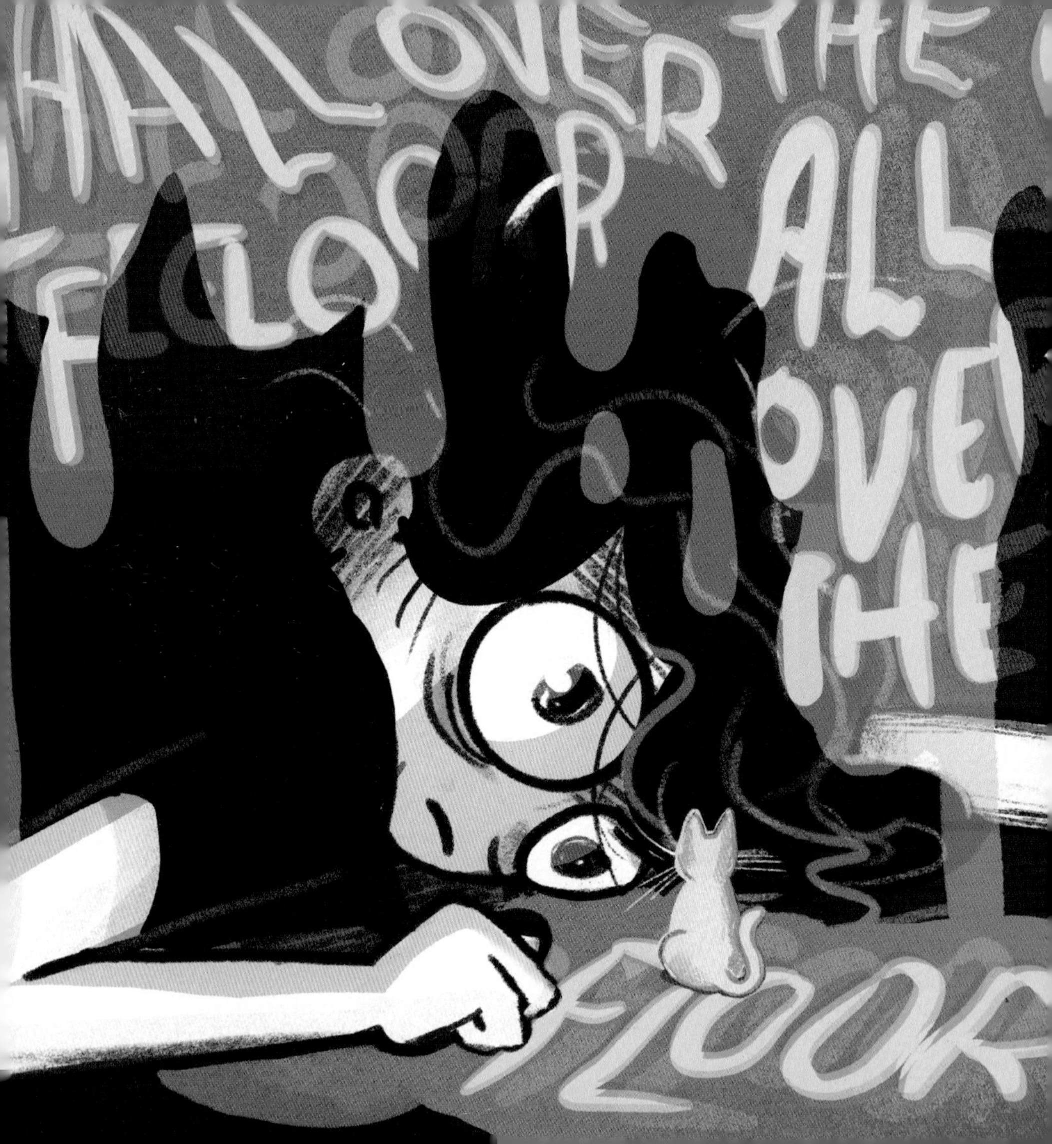
ALL OVER THE
FLOOR
ALL OVER THE
FLOOR

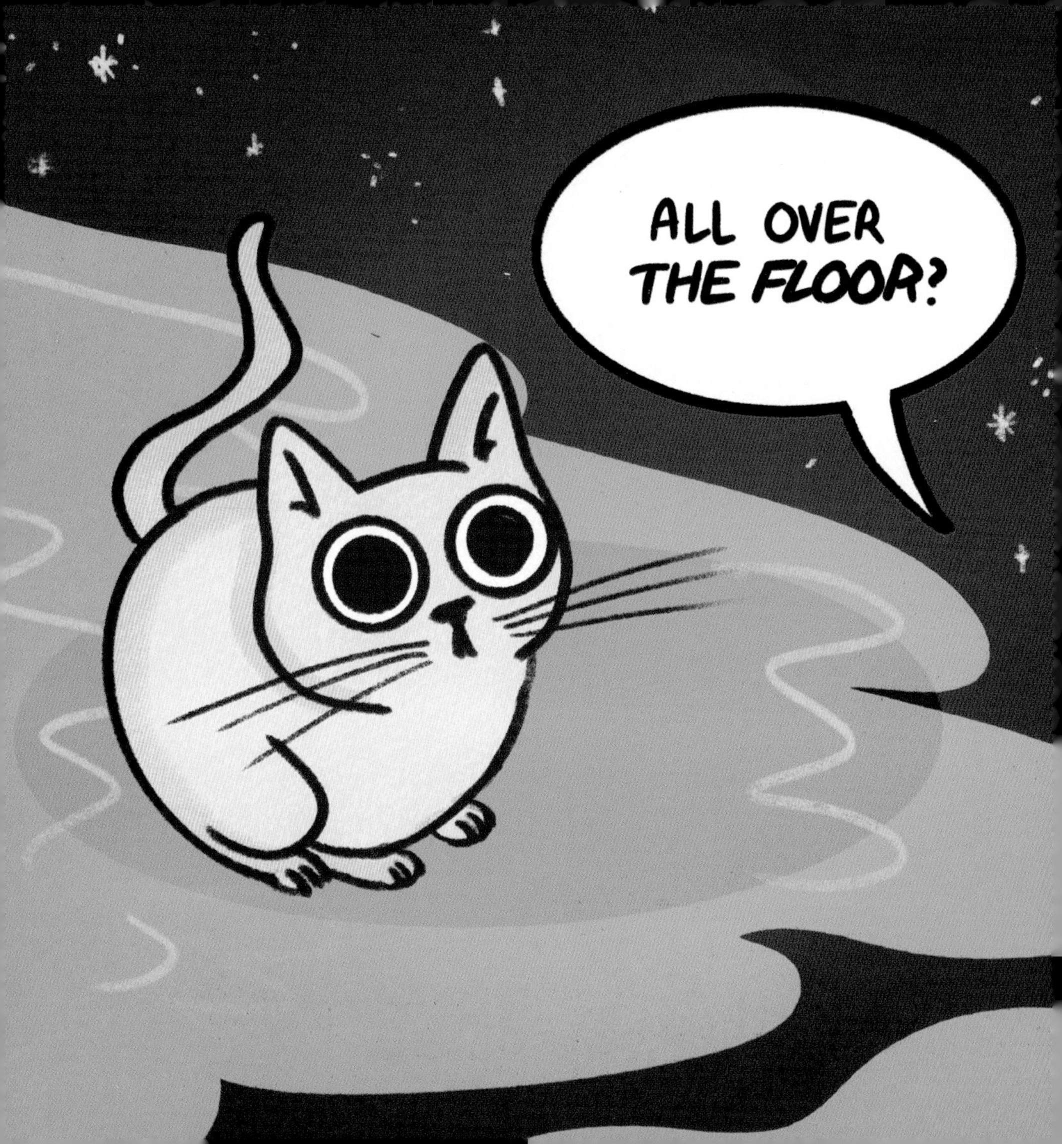
ALL OVER THE FLOOR?

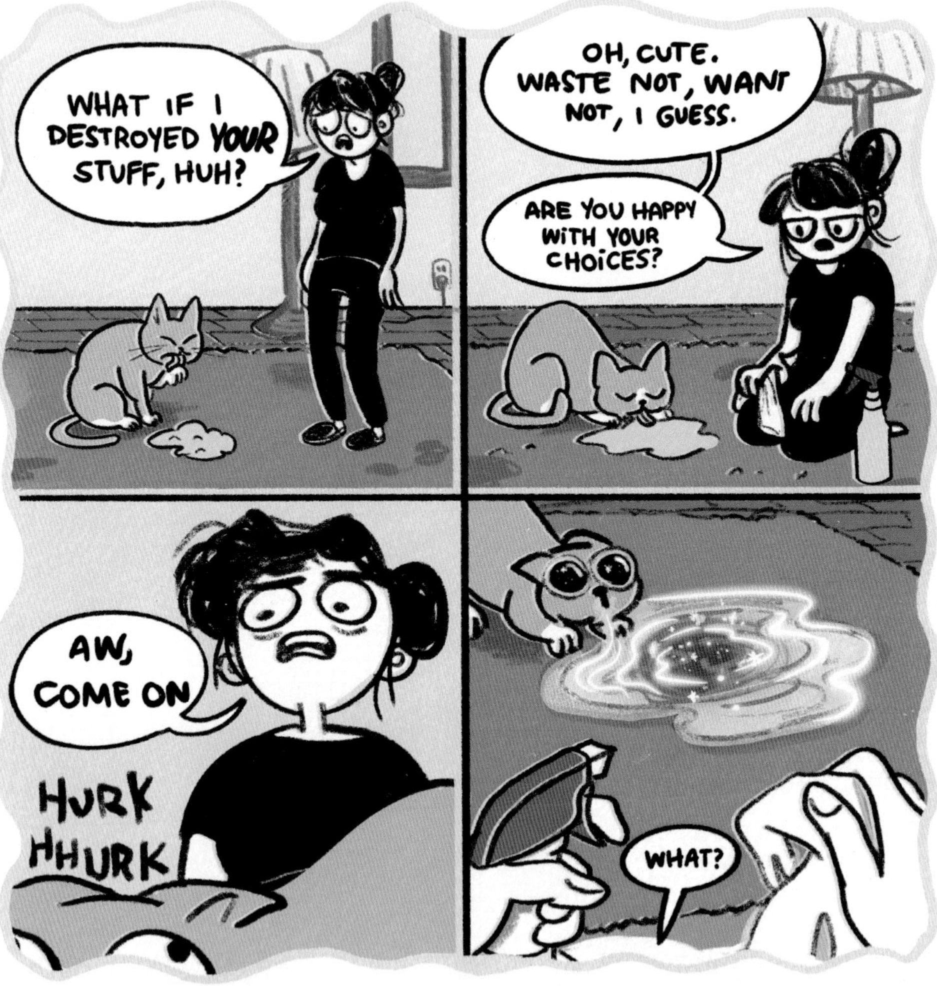
WHAT IF I DESTROYED YOUR STUFF, HUH?
OH, CUTE. WASTE NOT, WANT NOT, I GUESS.
ARE YOU HAPPY WITH YOUR CHOICES?
AW, COME ON
HURK HHURK
WHAT?

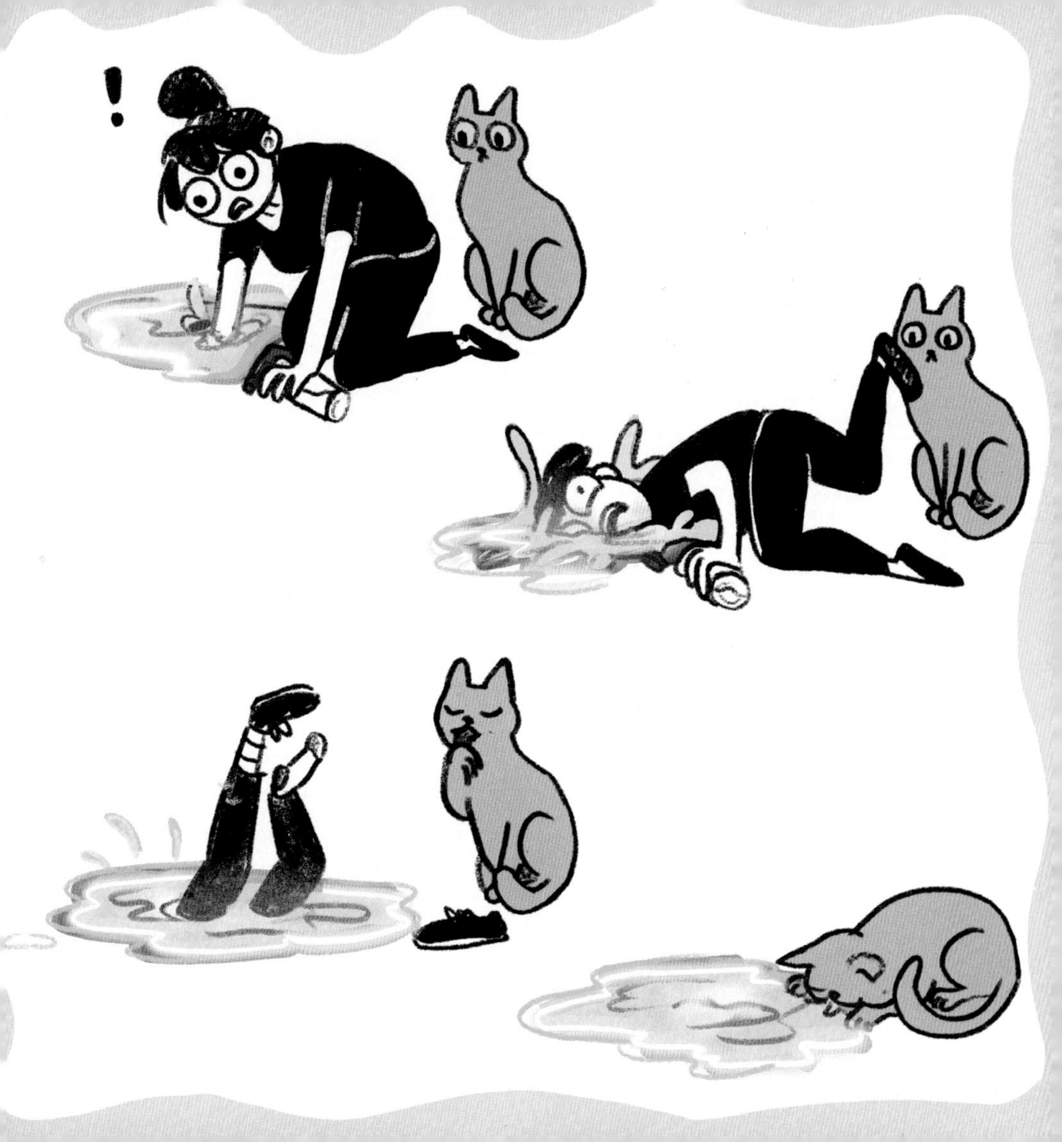
!

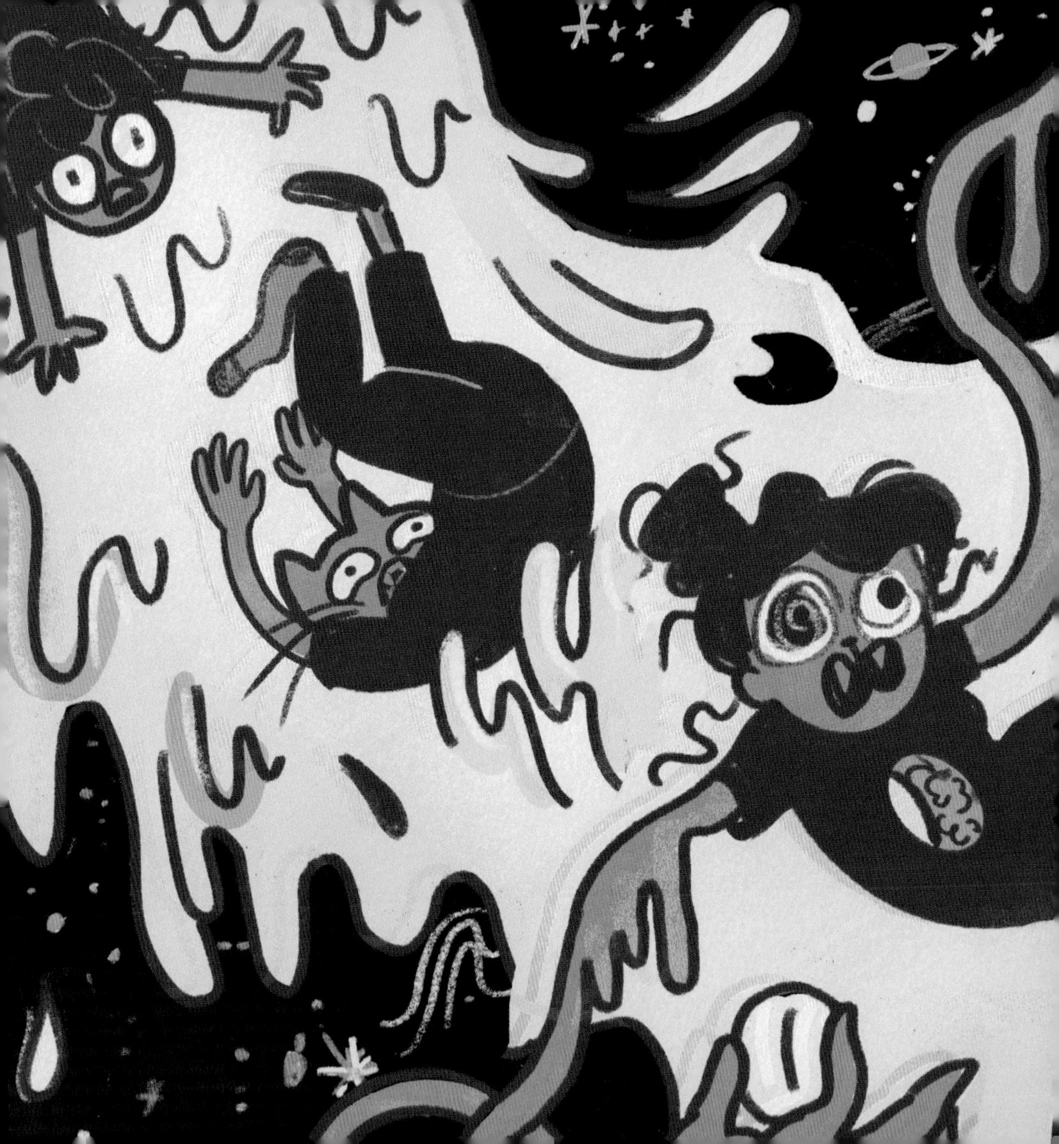

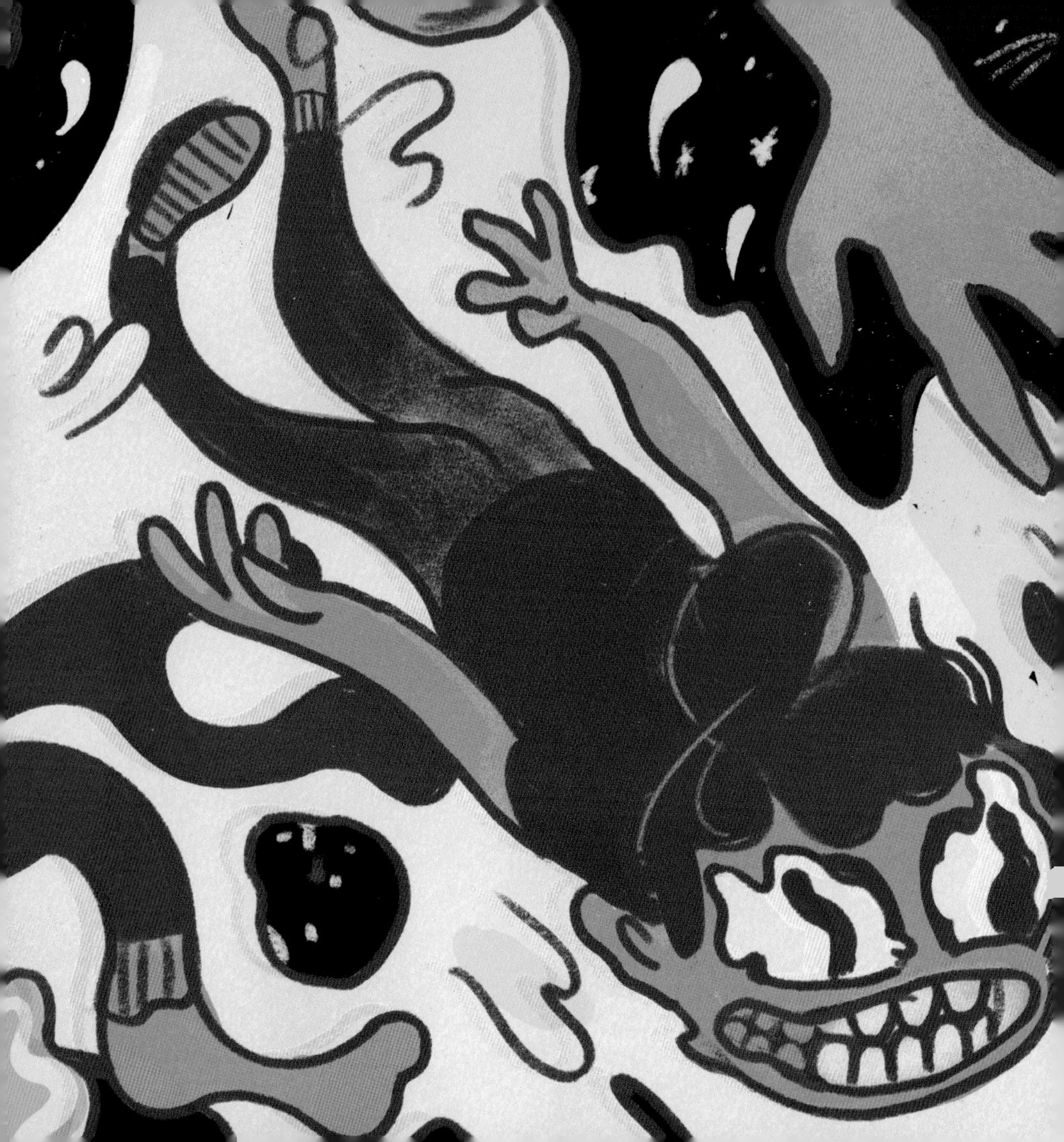

THUD
GUH-GUNK
GUH-GUNK
FWUMP

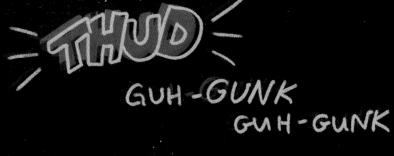

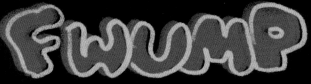

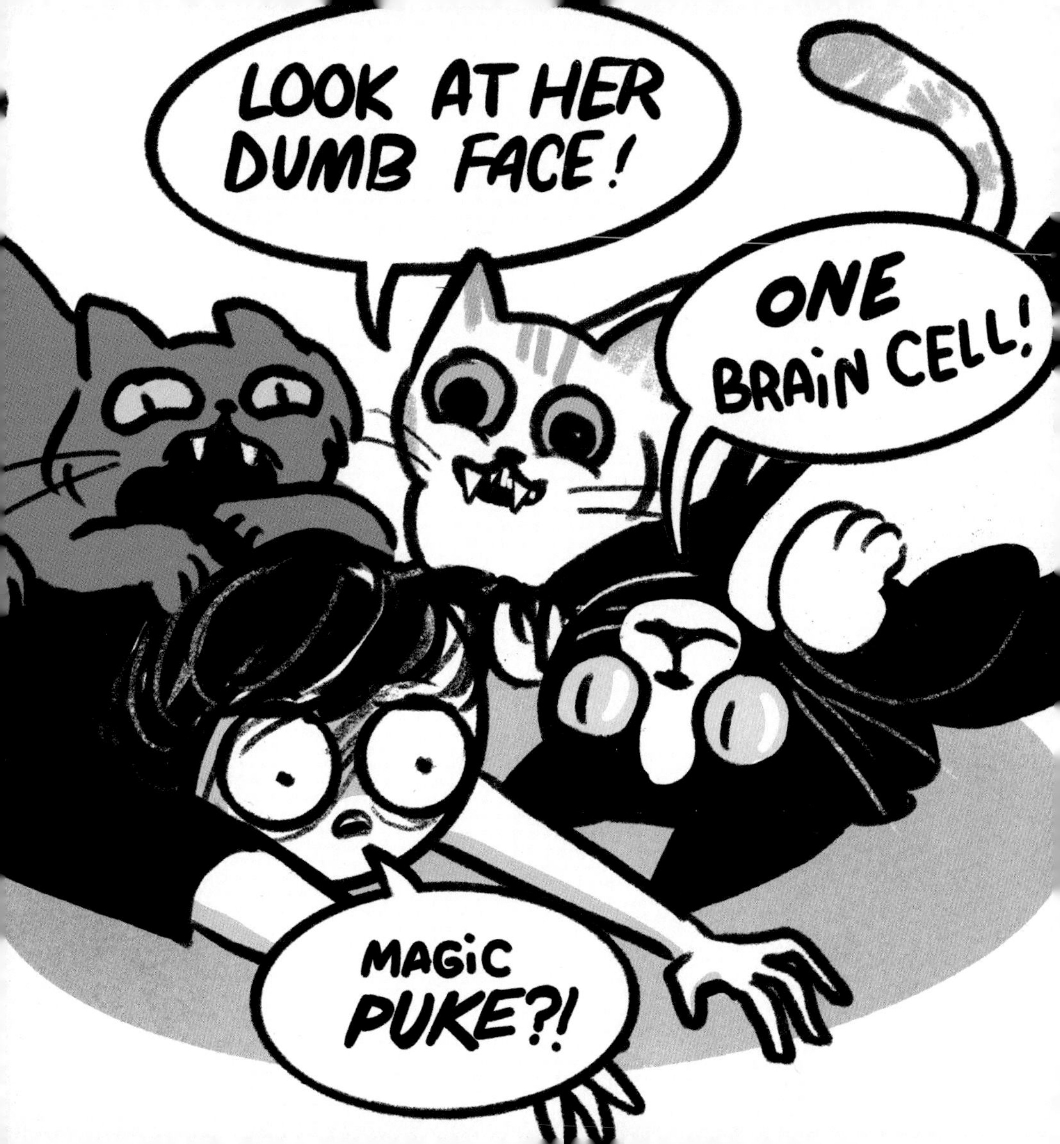
LOOK AT HER DUMB FACE!
ONE BRAIN CELL!
MAGIC PUKE?!

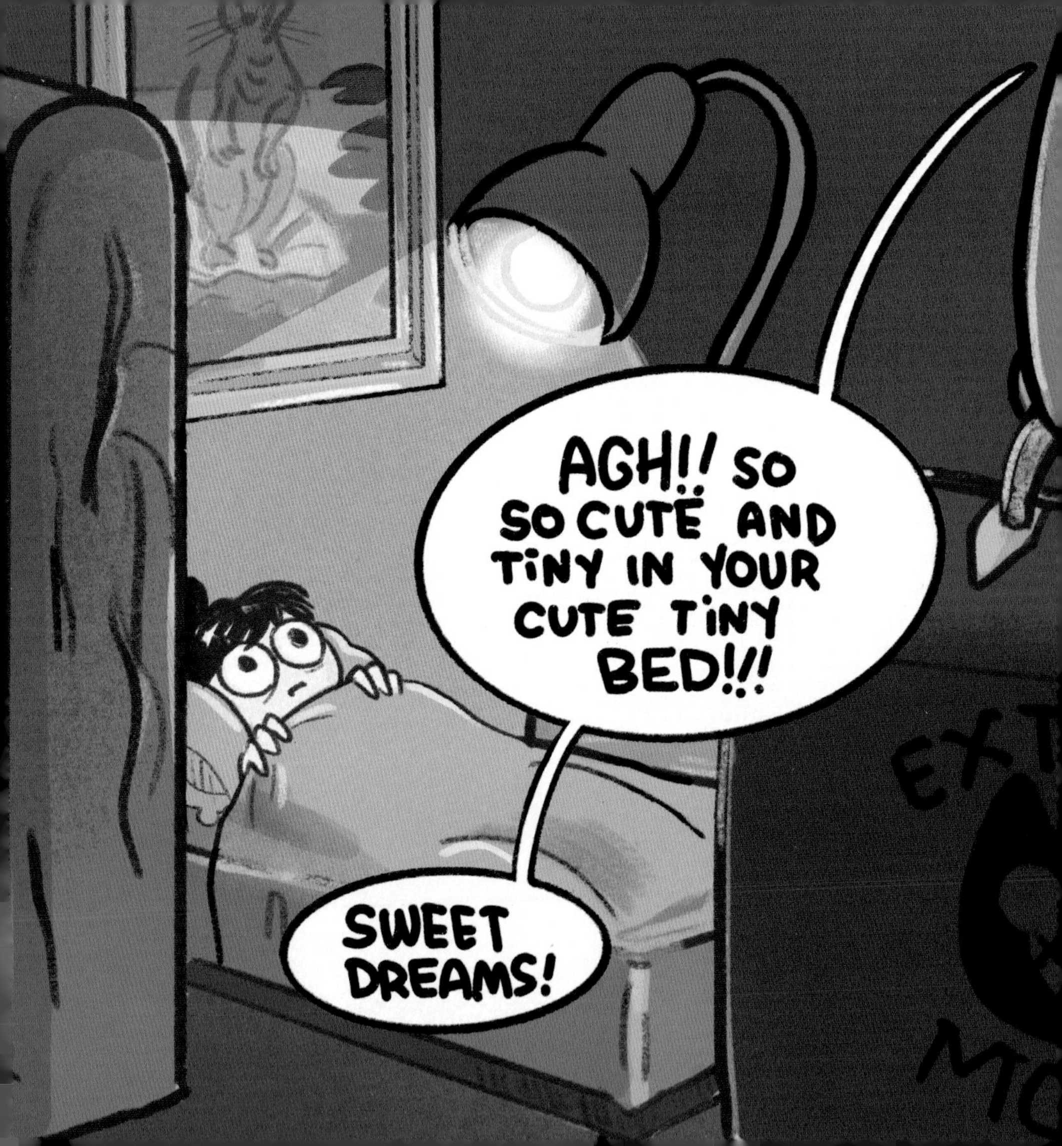
AGH!! SO SO CUTE AND TINY IN YOUR CUTE TINY BED!!!
SWEET DREAMS!

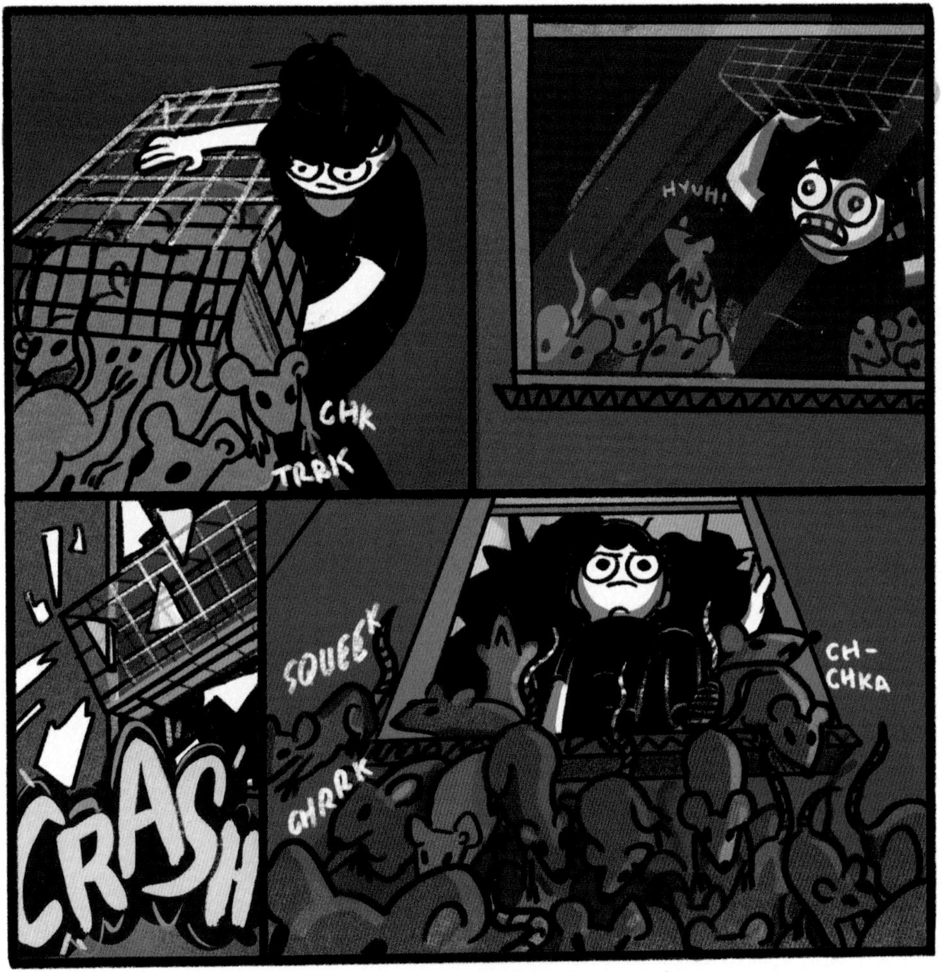
CHK
TRRK
HYUH!
CRASH
SQUEEK
CHRRK
CH-
CHKA

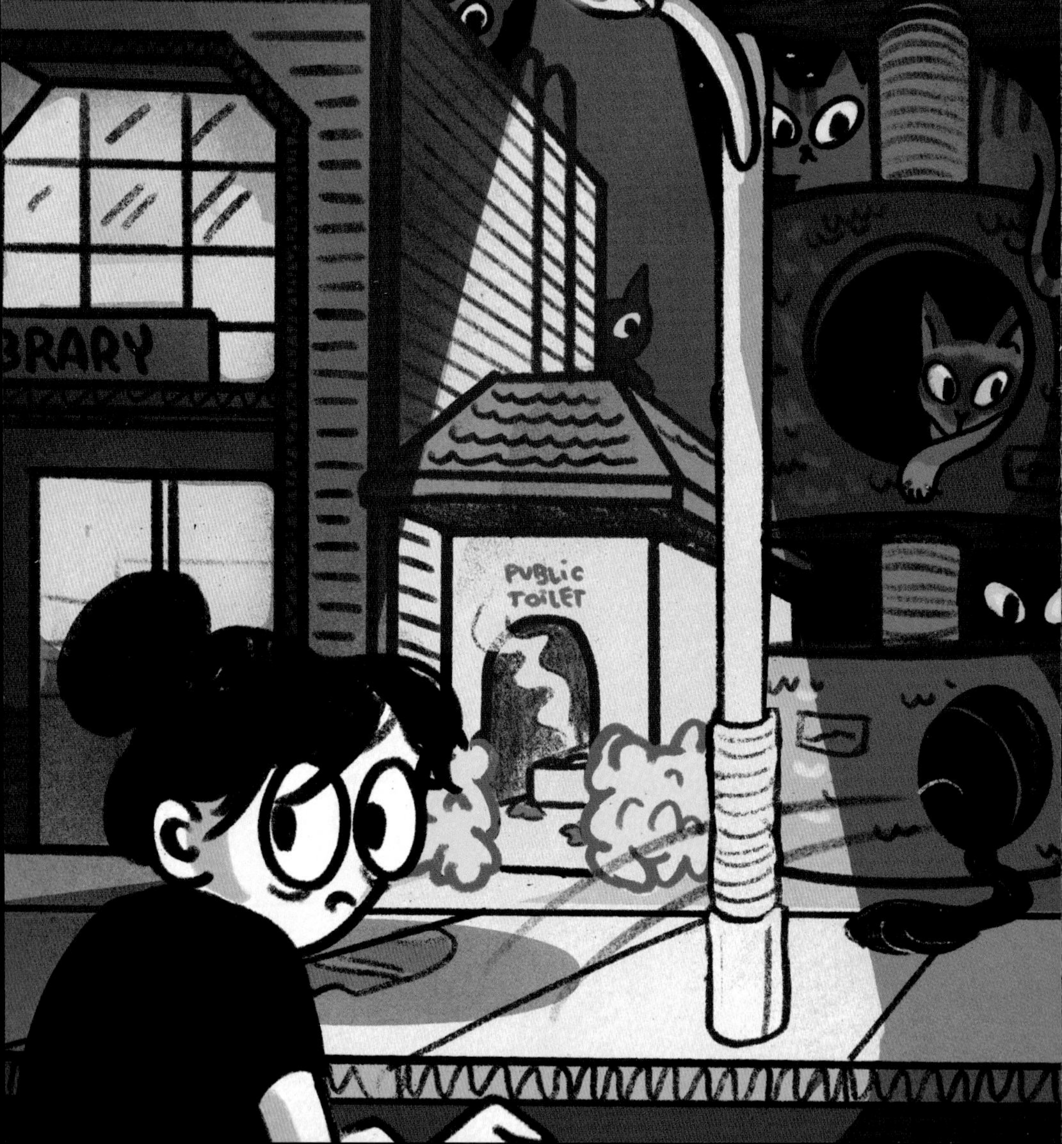
BRARY
PUBLIC
TOILET

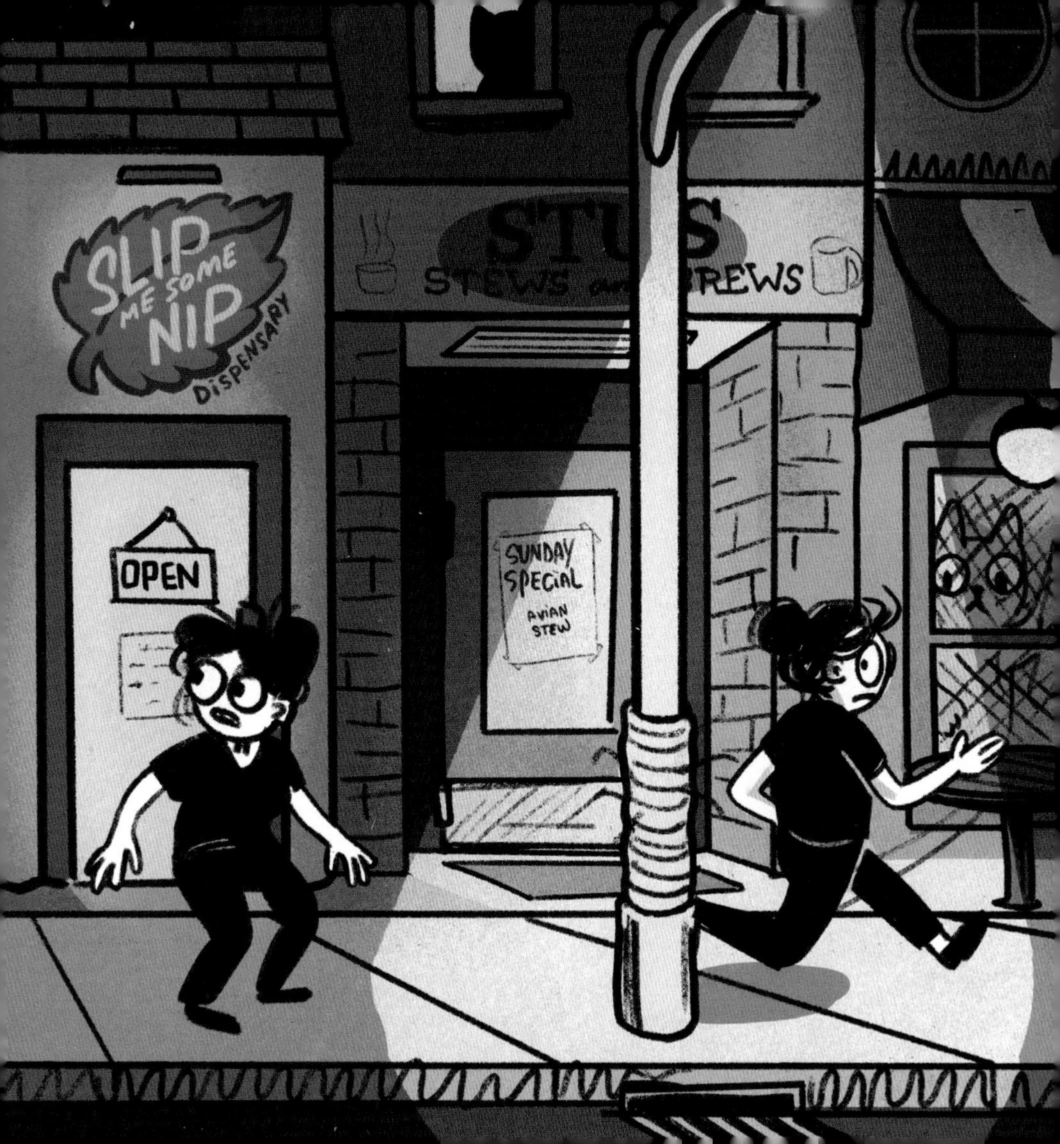
SLIP ME SOME NIP
DISPENSARY
OPEN
STU'S
STEWS
SUNDAY SPECIAL
AVIAN STEW

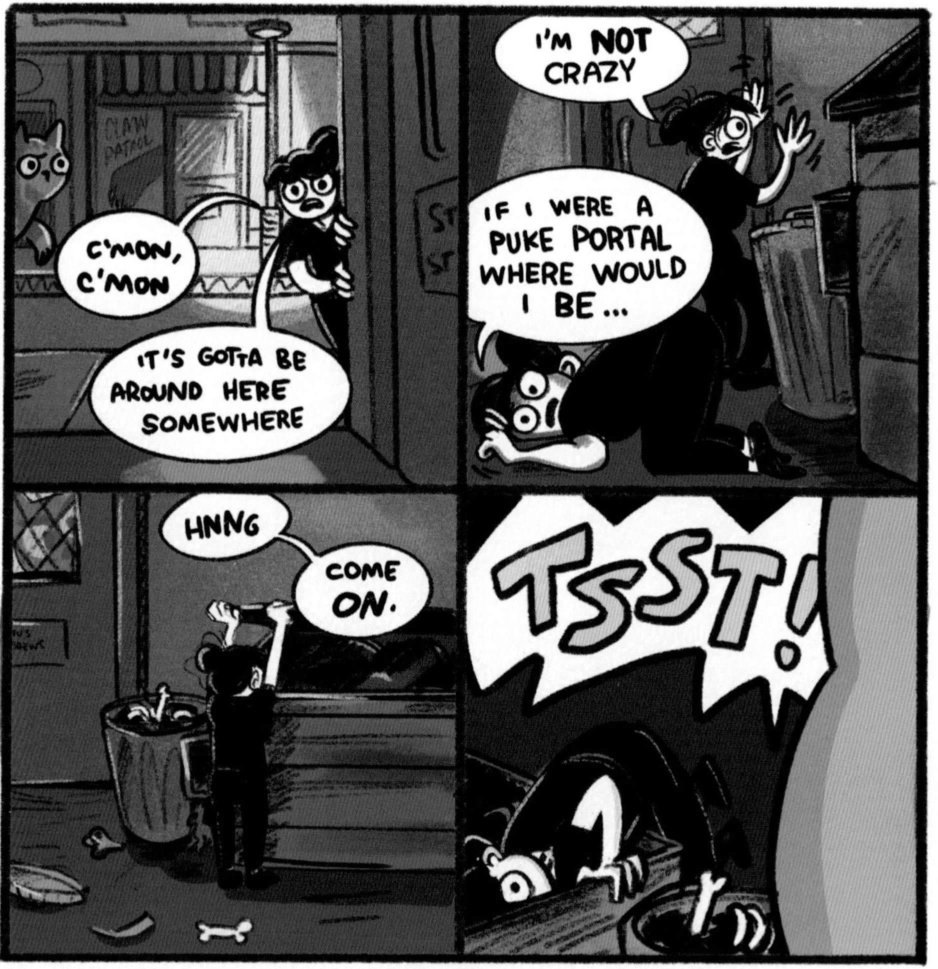
C'MON, C'MON
IT'S GOTTA BE AROUND HERE SOMEWHERE
I'M NOT CRAZY
IF I WERE A PUKE PORTAL WHERE WOULD I BE...
HNNG
COME ON.
TSST!

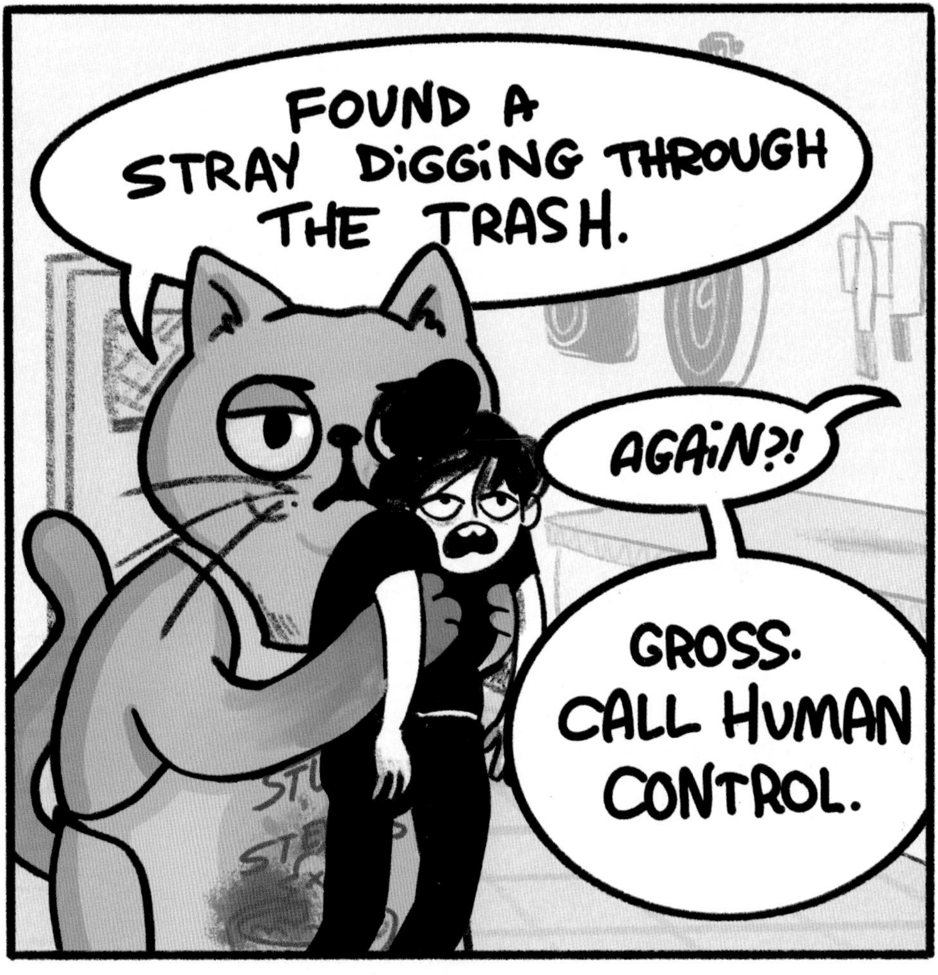
FOUND A STRAY DIGGING THROUGH THE TRASH.
AGAIN?!
GROSS. CALL HUMAN CONTROL.

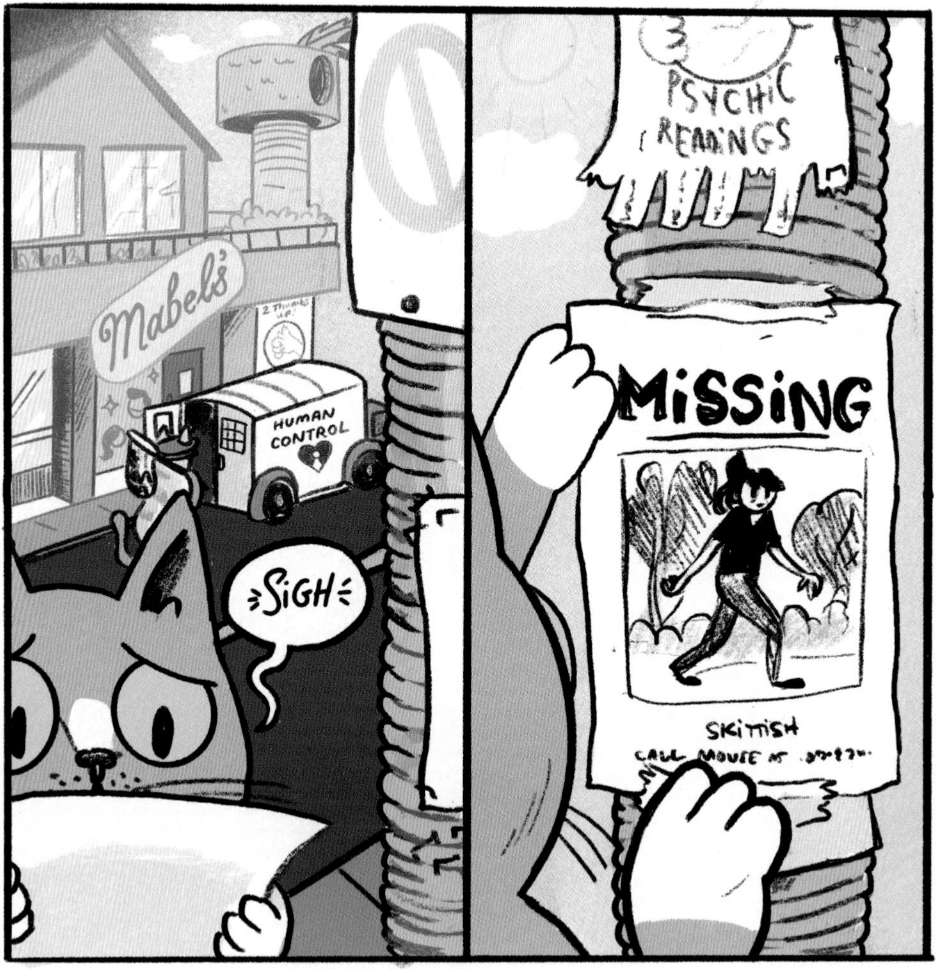
Mabel's
2 THUMBS UP!
HUMAN CONTROL
SIGH
PSYCHIC READINGS
MISSING
SKITTISH
CALL MOUSE AT

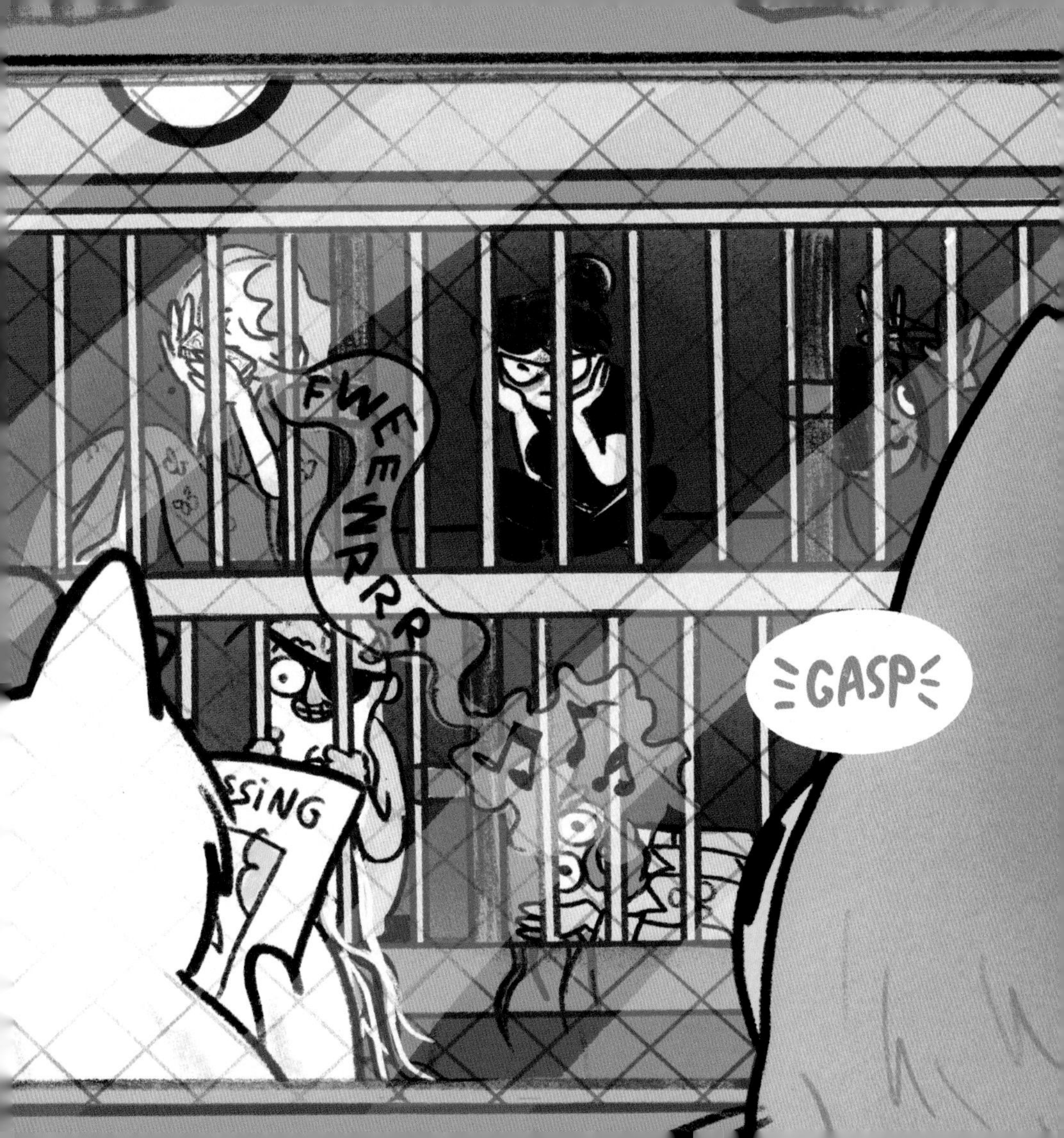
FWEEWRRRR
GASP
SSING

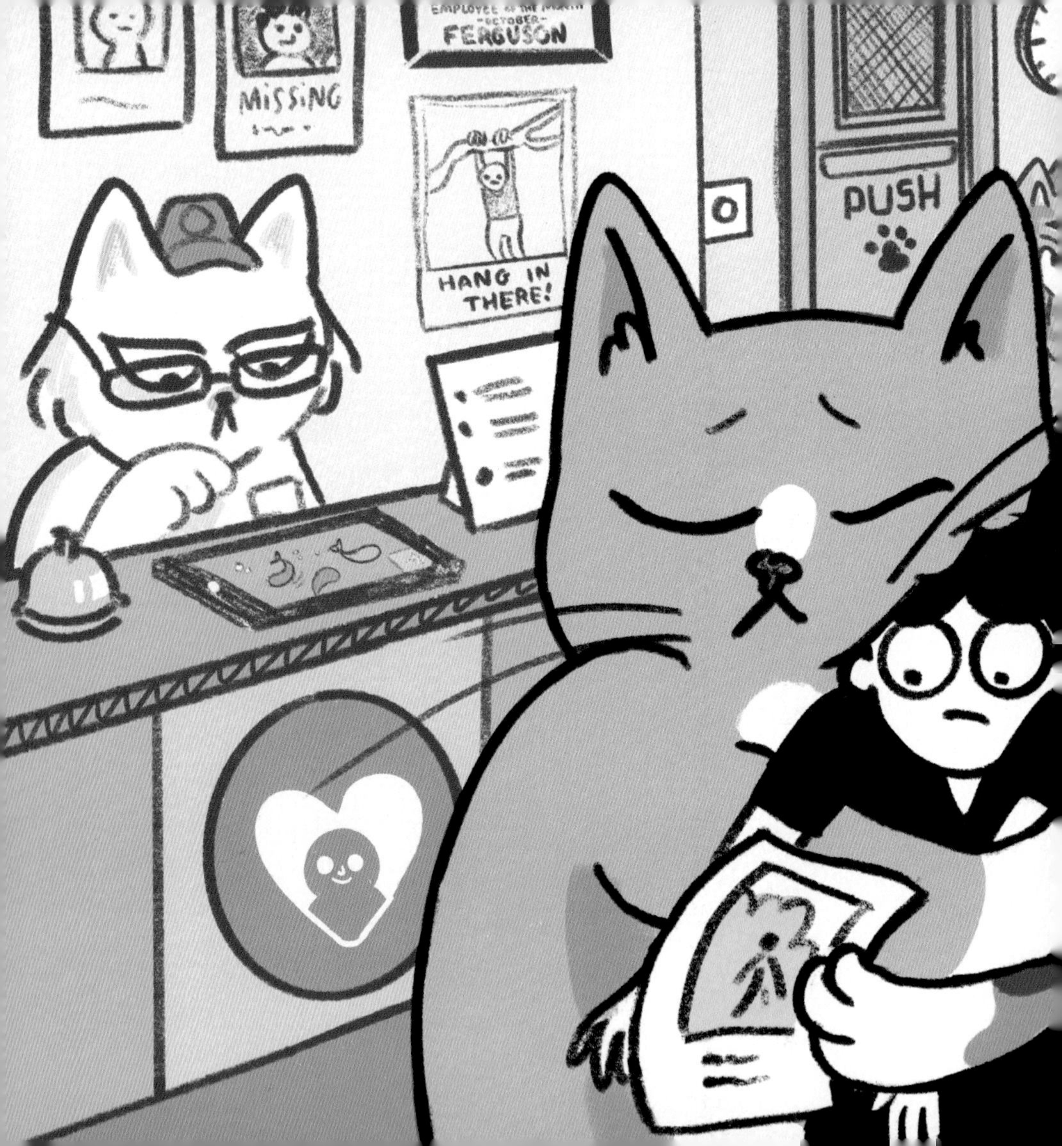
EMPLOYEE
-OCTOBER-
FERGUSON
MISSING
HANG IN THERE!
PUSH

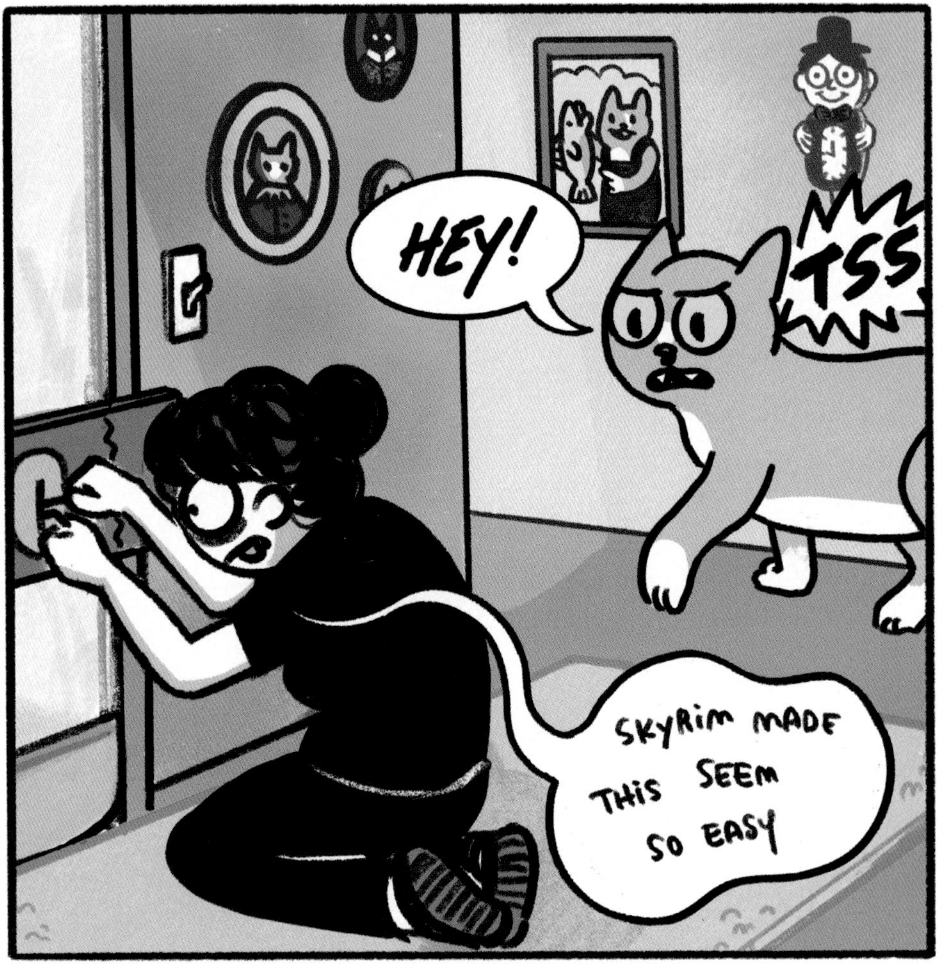
HEY!
TSS
SKYRIM MADE THIS SEEM SO EASY

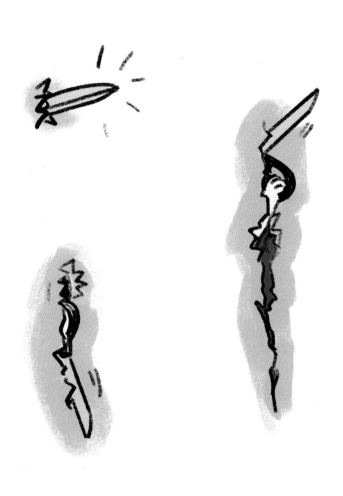

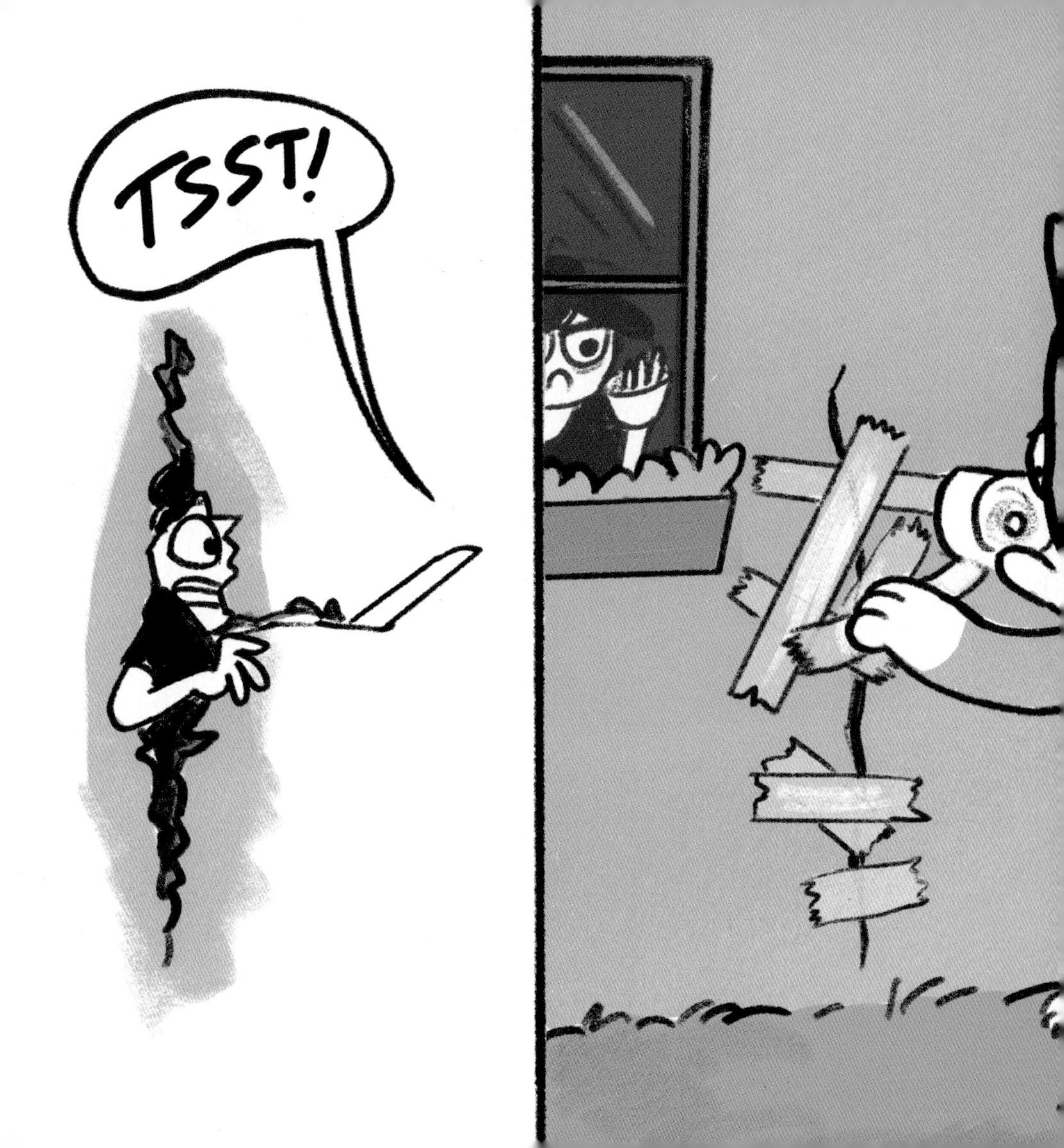
TSST!

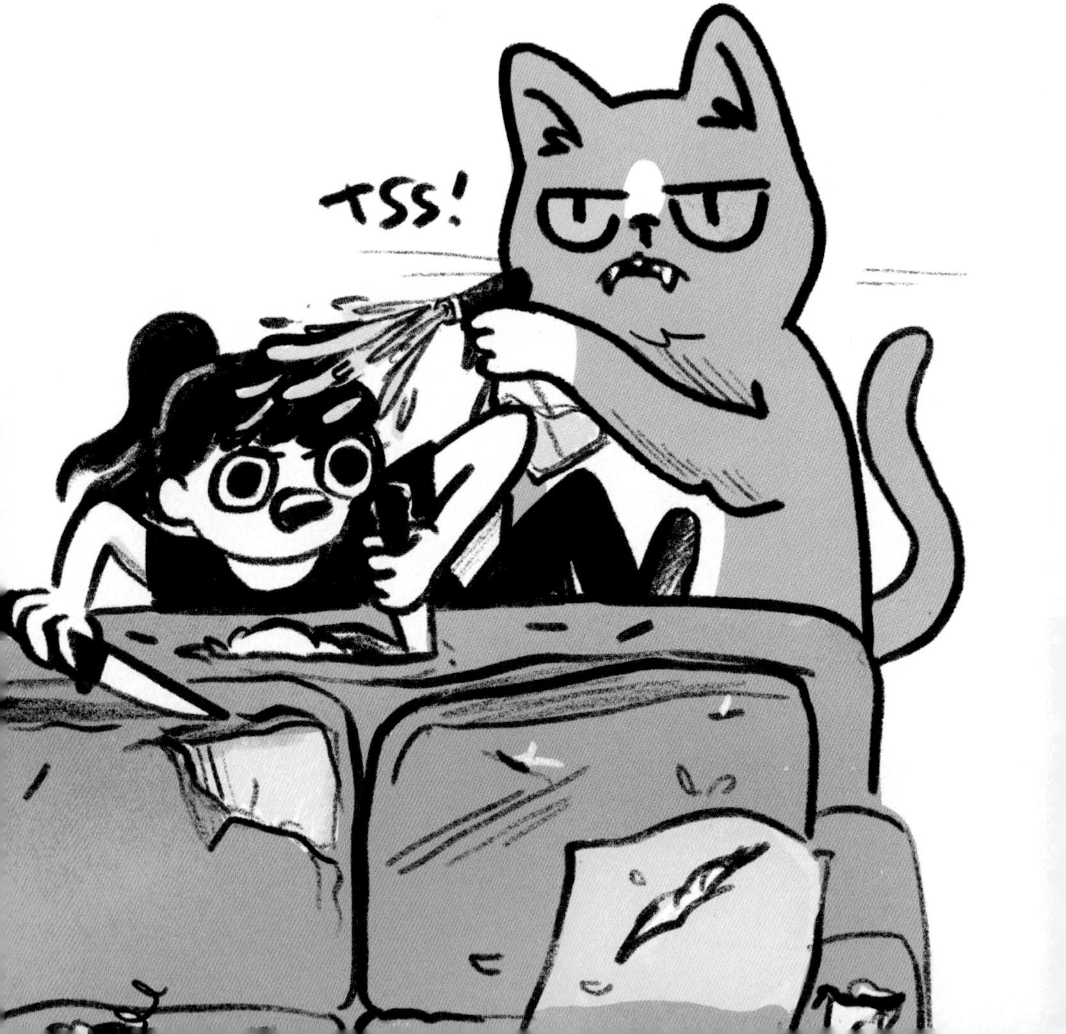
TSS!

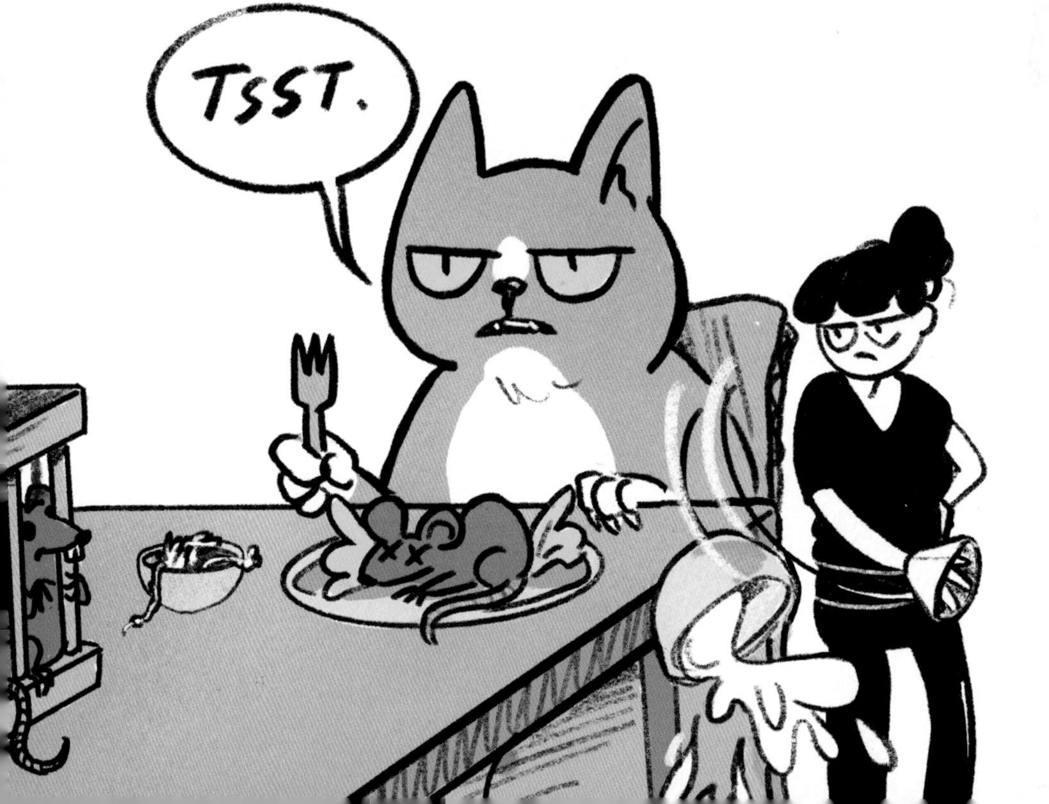
TSST.

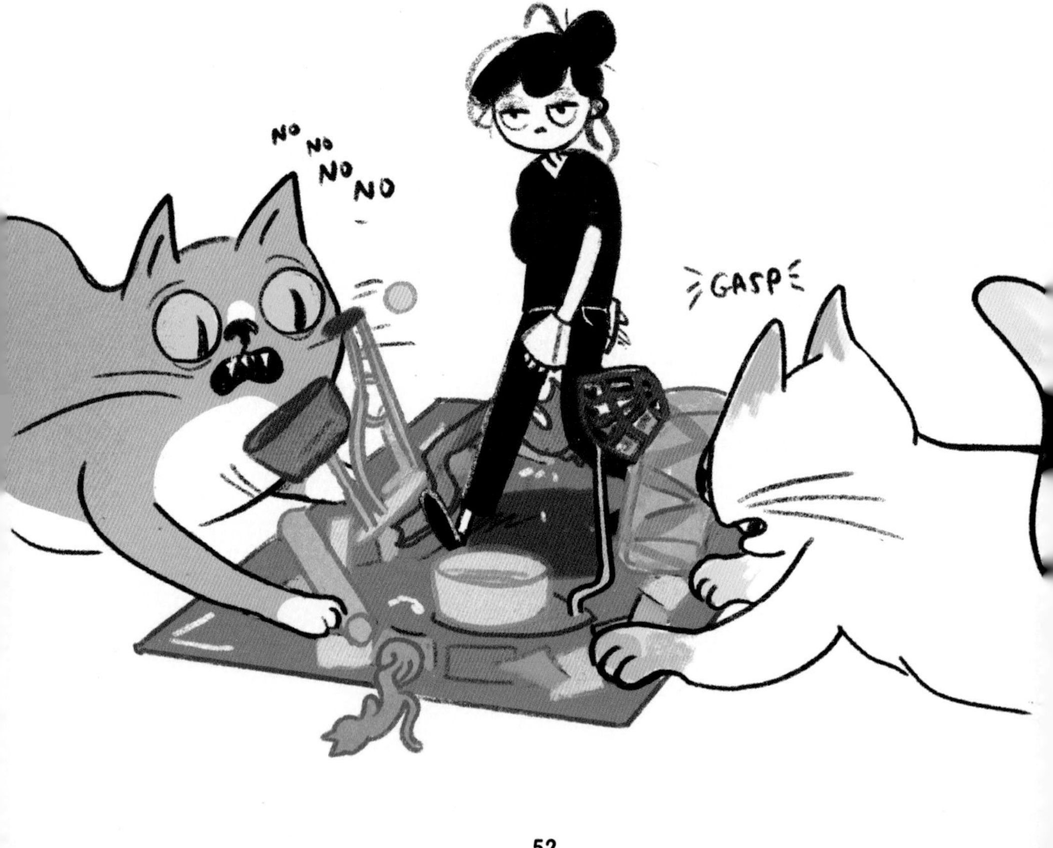
NO NO NO NO
GASP

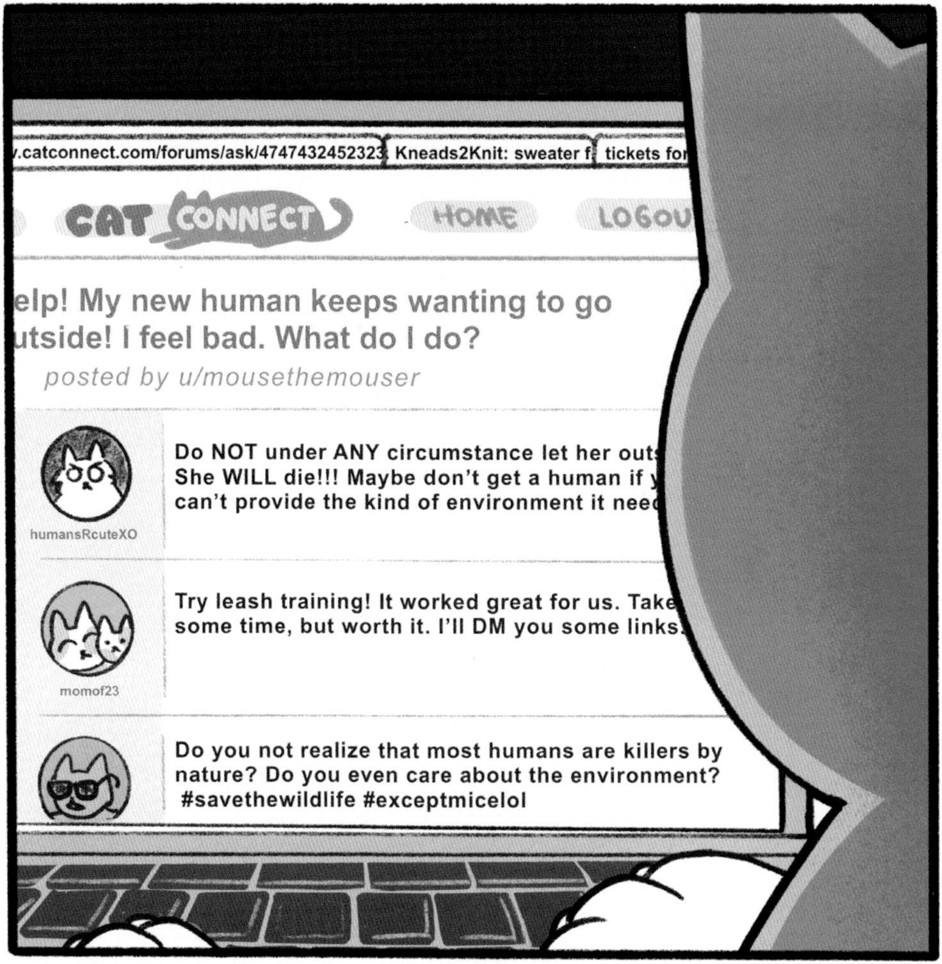
.catconnect.com/forums/ask/4747432452323
Kneads2Knit: sweater f
tickets fo
CAT CONNECT
HOME
LOGOU
elp! My new human keeps wanting to go
utside! I feel bad. What do I do?
posted by u/mousethemouser
humansRcuteXO
Do NOT under ANY circumstance let her out
She WILL die!!! Maybe don't get a human if y
can't provide the kind of environment it need
momof23
Try leash training! It worked great for us. Take
some time, but worth it. I'll DM you some links
Do you not realize that most humans are killers by
nature? Do you even care about the environment?
#savethewildlife #exceptmicelol

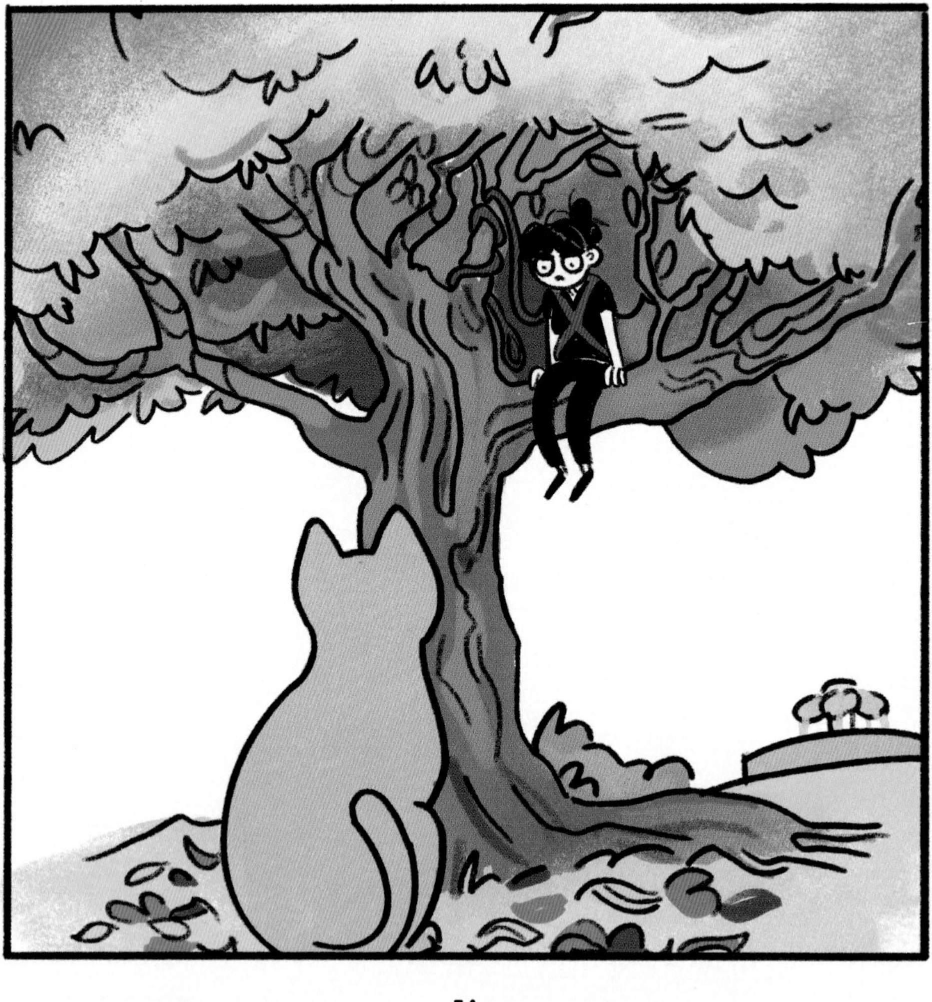

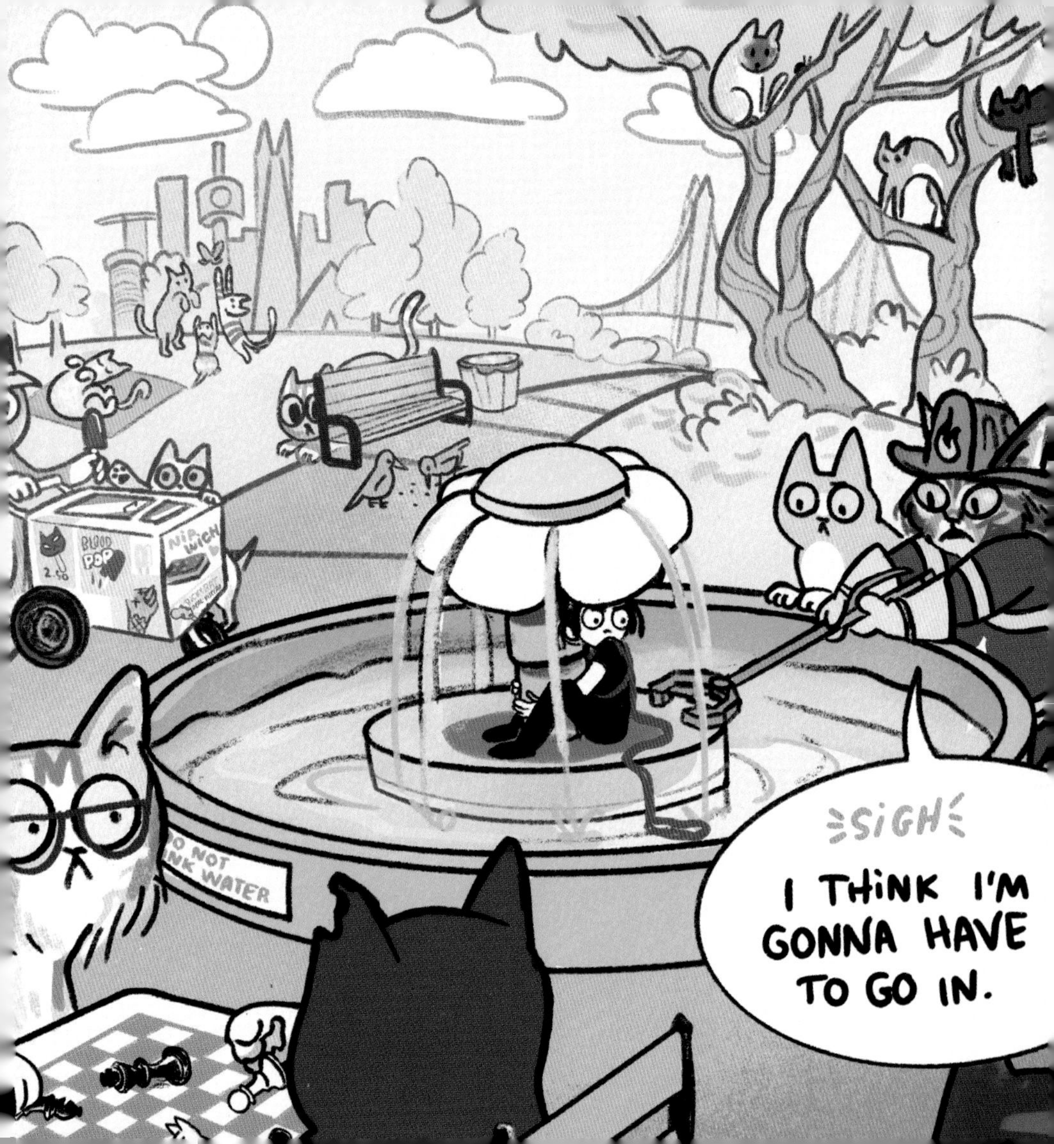
BLOOD POP
SIGH
I THINK I'M GONNA HAVE TO GO IN.

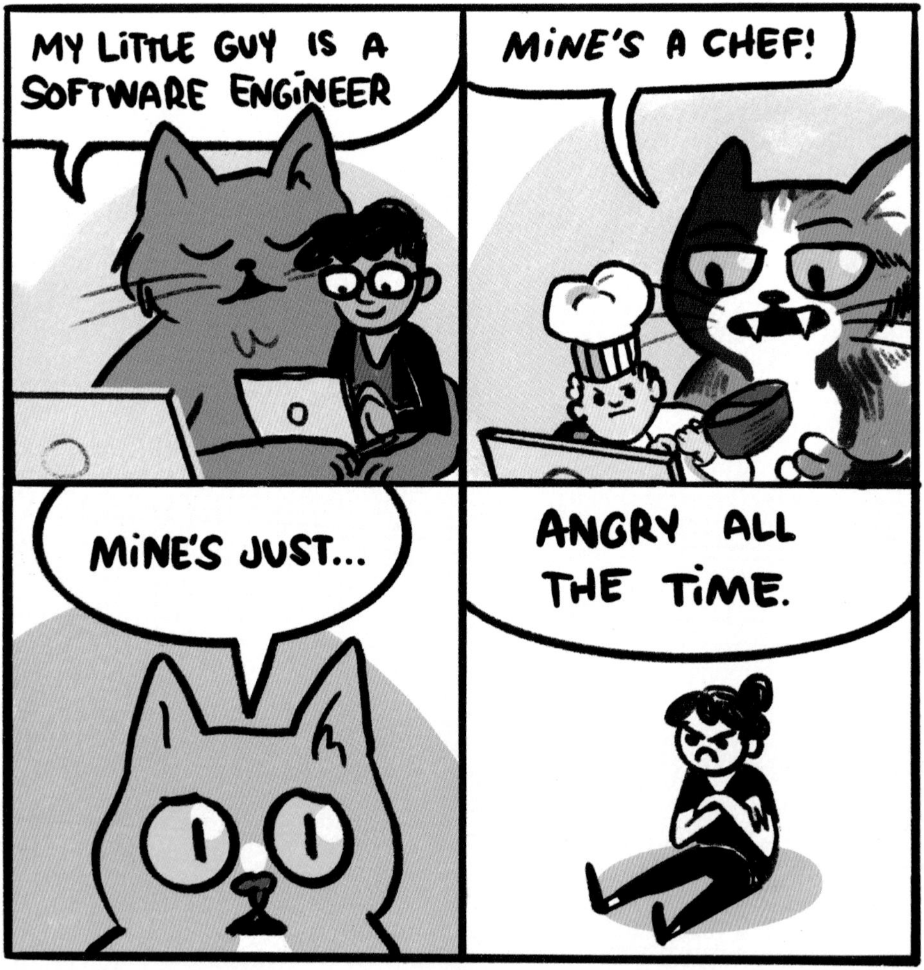
MY LITTLE GUY IS A SOFTWARE ENGINEER
MINE'S A CHEF!
MINE'S JUST...
ANGRY ALL THE TIME.

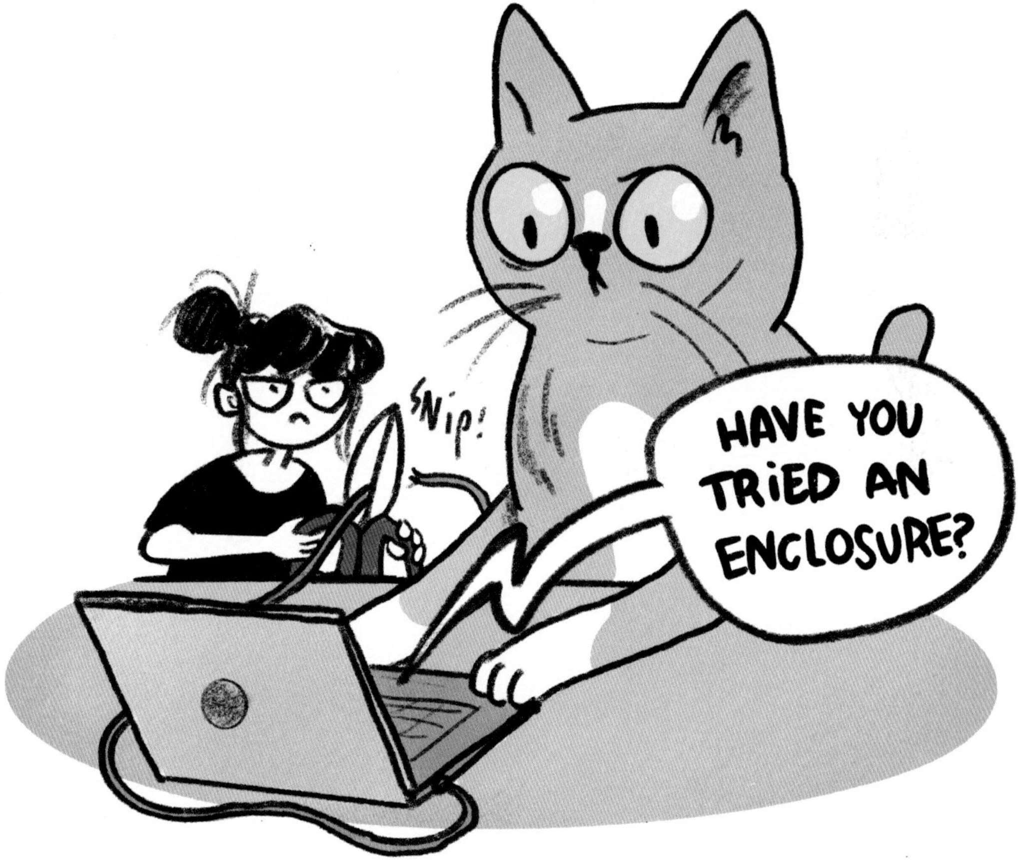
SNip!
HAVE YOU TRiED AN ENCLOSURE?

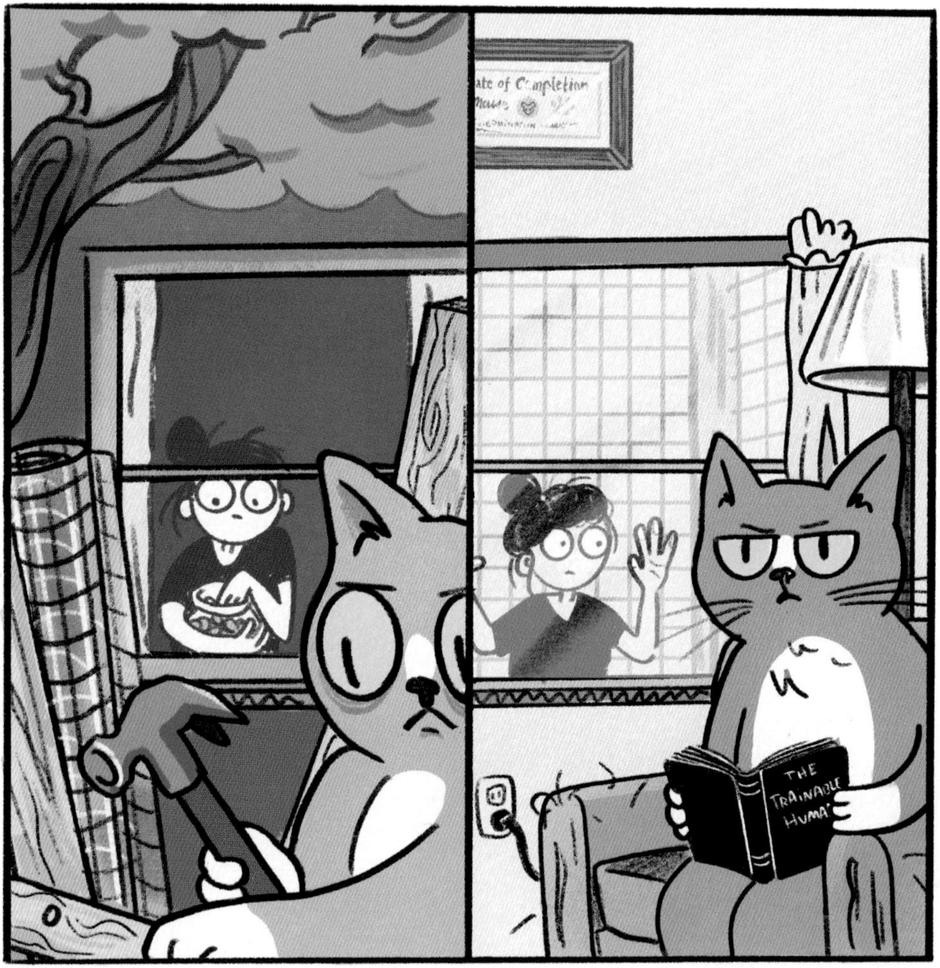
THE TRAINABLE

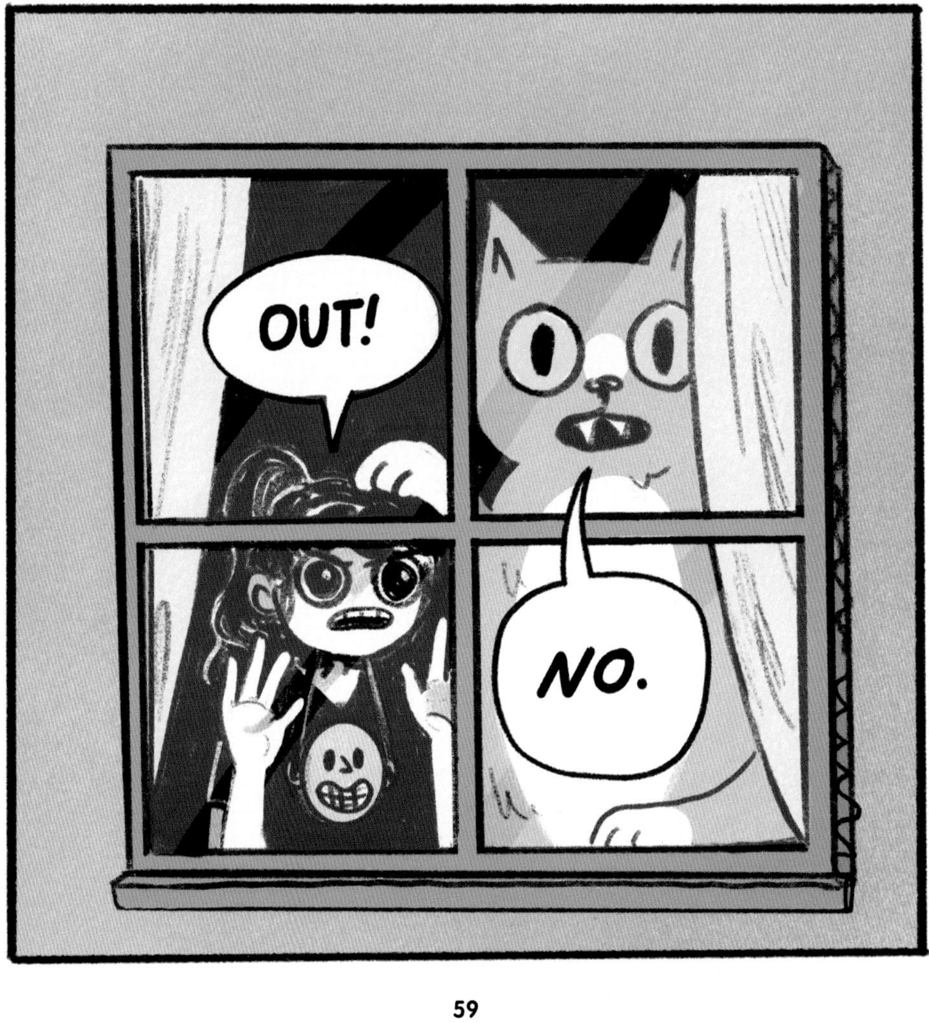
OUT!
NO.

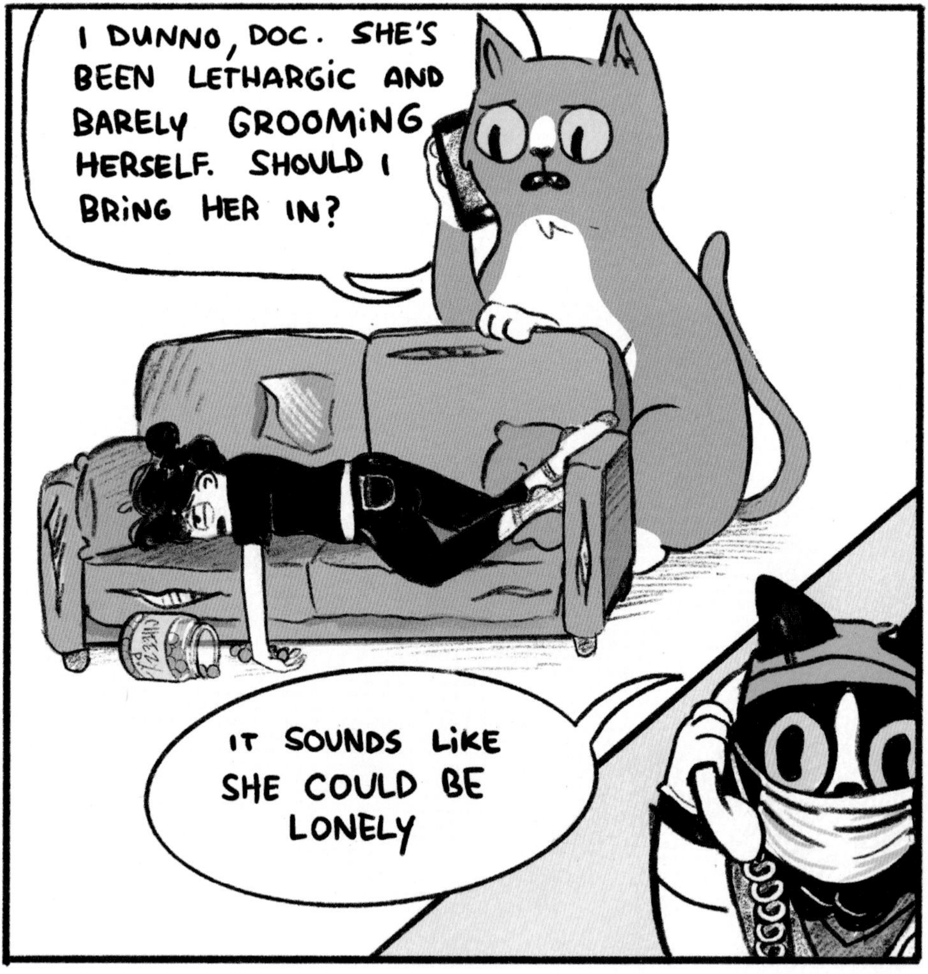
I DUNNO, DOC. SHE'S BEEN LETHARGIC AND BARELY GROOMING HERSELF. SHOULD I BRING HER IN?
IT SOUNDS LIKE SHE COULD BE LONELY

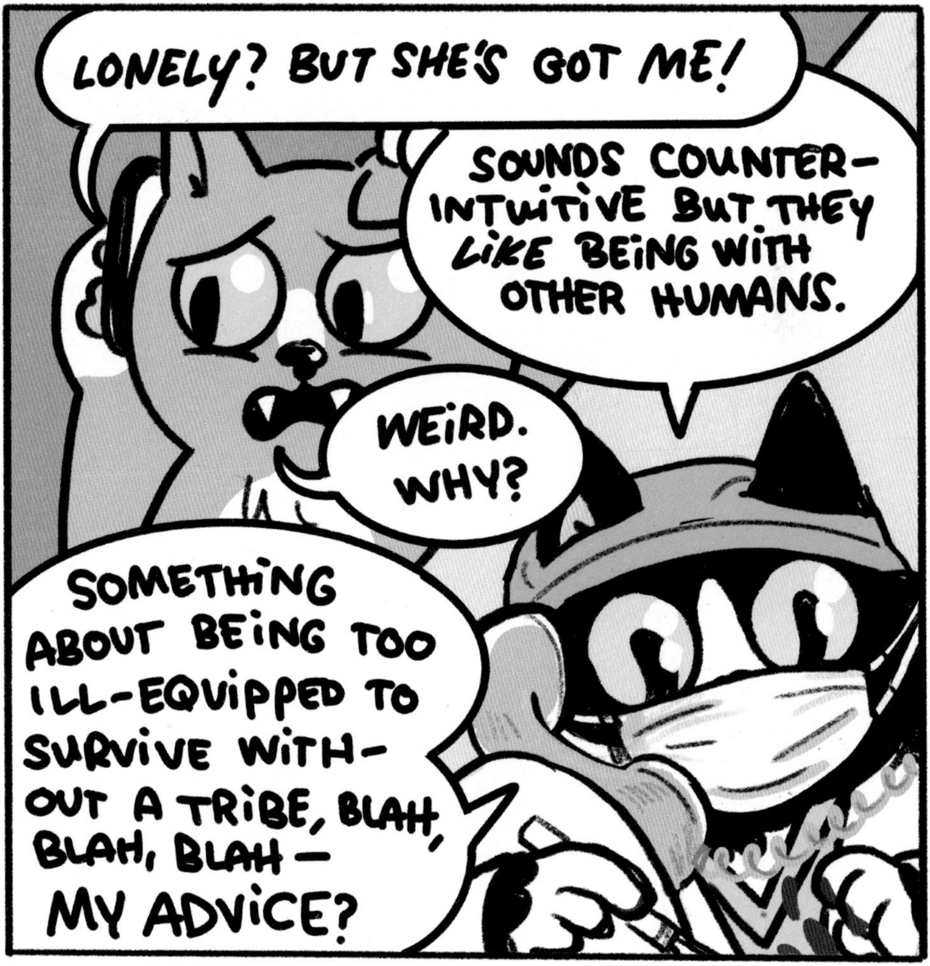
LONELY? BUT SHE'S GOT ME!
SOUNDS COUNTER-INTUITIVE BUT THEY LIKE BEING WITH OTHER HUMANS.
WEIRD. WHY?
SOMETHING ABOUT BEING TOO ILL-EQUIPPED TO SURVIVE WITH-OUT A TRIBE, BLAH, BLAH, BLAH — MY ADVICE?

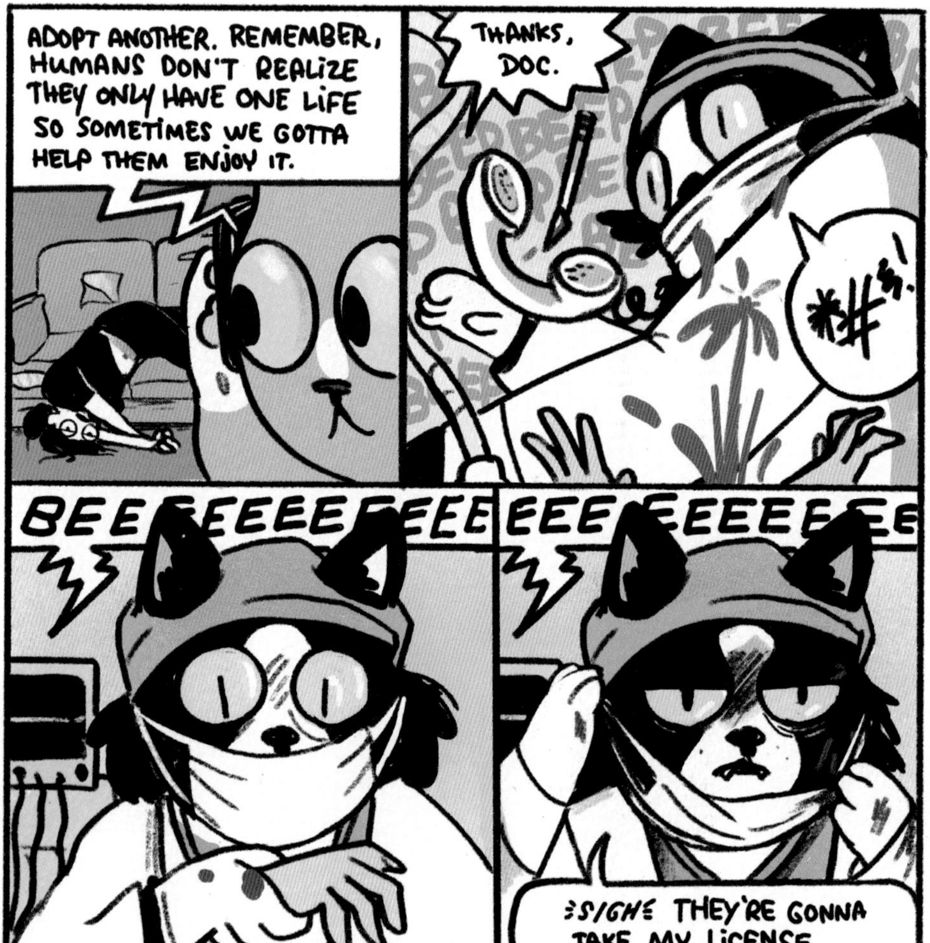
ADOPT ANOTHER. REMEMBER, HUMANS DON'T REALIZE THEY ONLY HAVE ONE LIFE SO SOMETIMES WE GOTTA HELP THEM ENJOY IT.
THANKS, DOC.
BEEP BEEP BEEP
*#$!
BEEEEEEEEEEEEEEEEEEEEEEE
SIGH THEY'RE GONNA TAKE MY LICENSE.

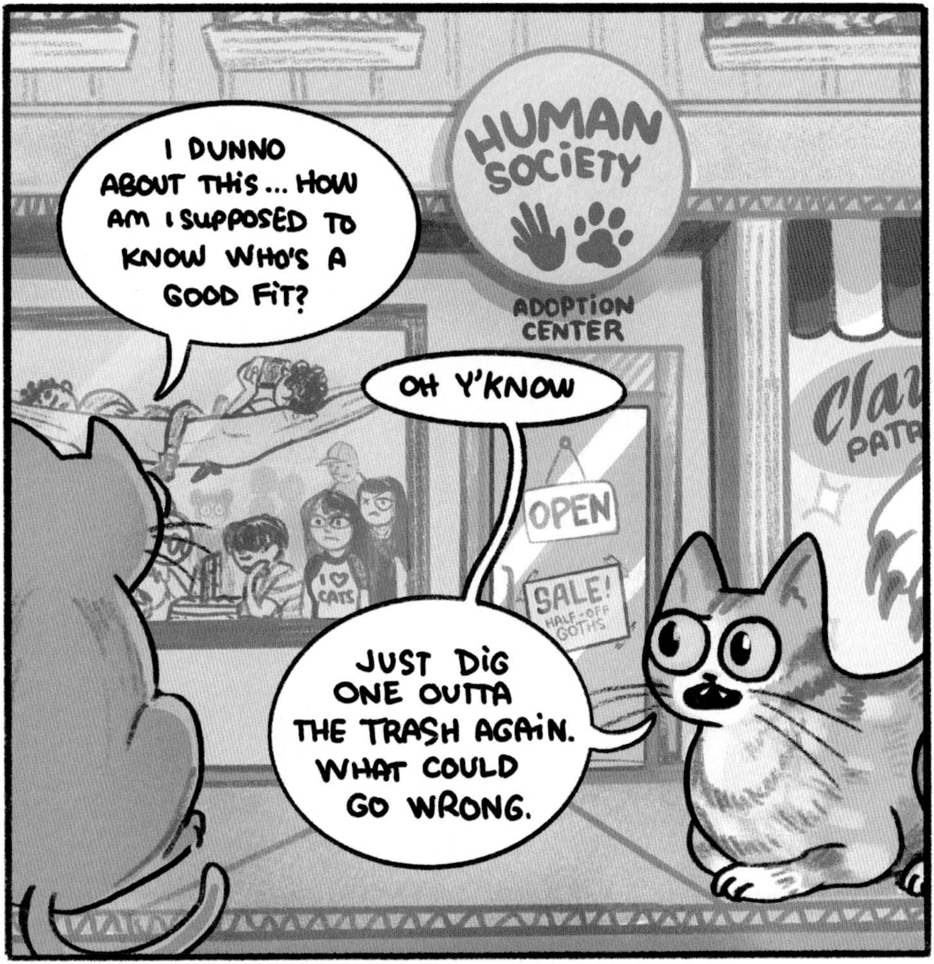
HUMAN SOCIETY
ADOPTION CENTER
I DUNNO ABOUT THIS... HOW AM I SUPPOSED TO KNOW WHO'S A GOOD FIT?
OH Y'KNOW
JUST DIG ONE OUTTA THE TRASH AGAIN. WHAT COULD GO WRONG.
OPEN
SALE! HALF-OFF GOTHS
I ♥ CATS

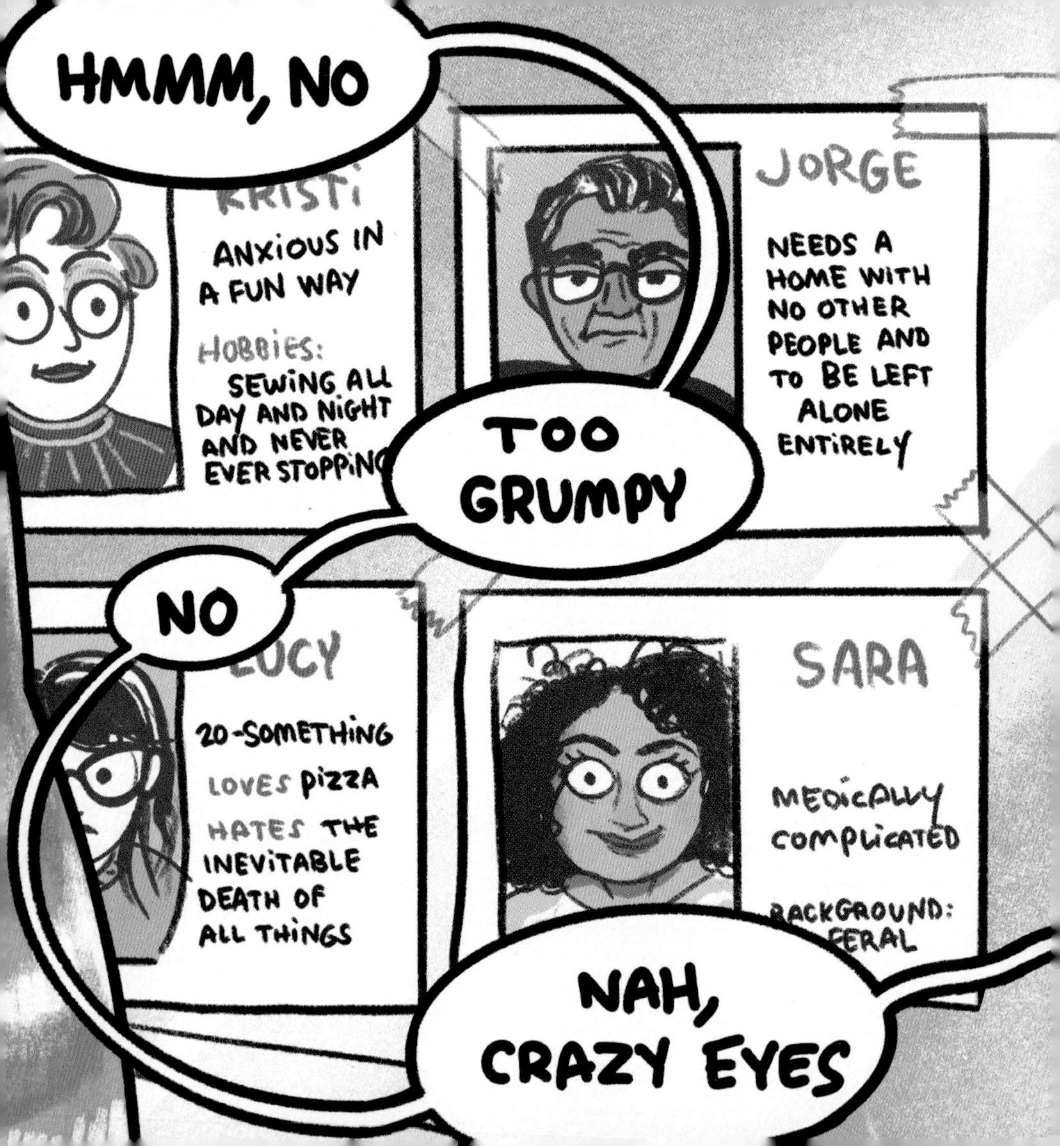
HMMM, NO
KRISTI
ANXIOUS IN A FUN WAY
HOBBIES:
SEWING ALL DAY AND NIGHT AND NEVER EVER STOPPING
JORGE
NEEDS A HOME WITH NO OTHER PEOPLE AND TO BE LEFT ALONE ENTIRELY
TOO GRUMPY
NO
20-SOMETHING
LOVES PIZZA
HATES THE INEVITABLE DEATH OF ALL THINGS
SARA
MEDICALLY COMPLICATED
BACKGROUND:
FERAL
NAH, CRAZY EYES

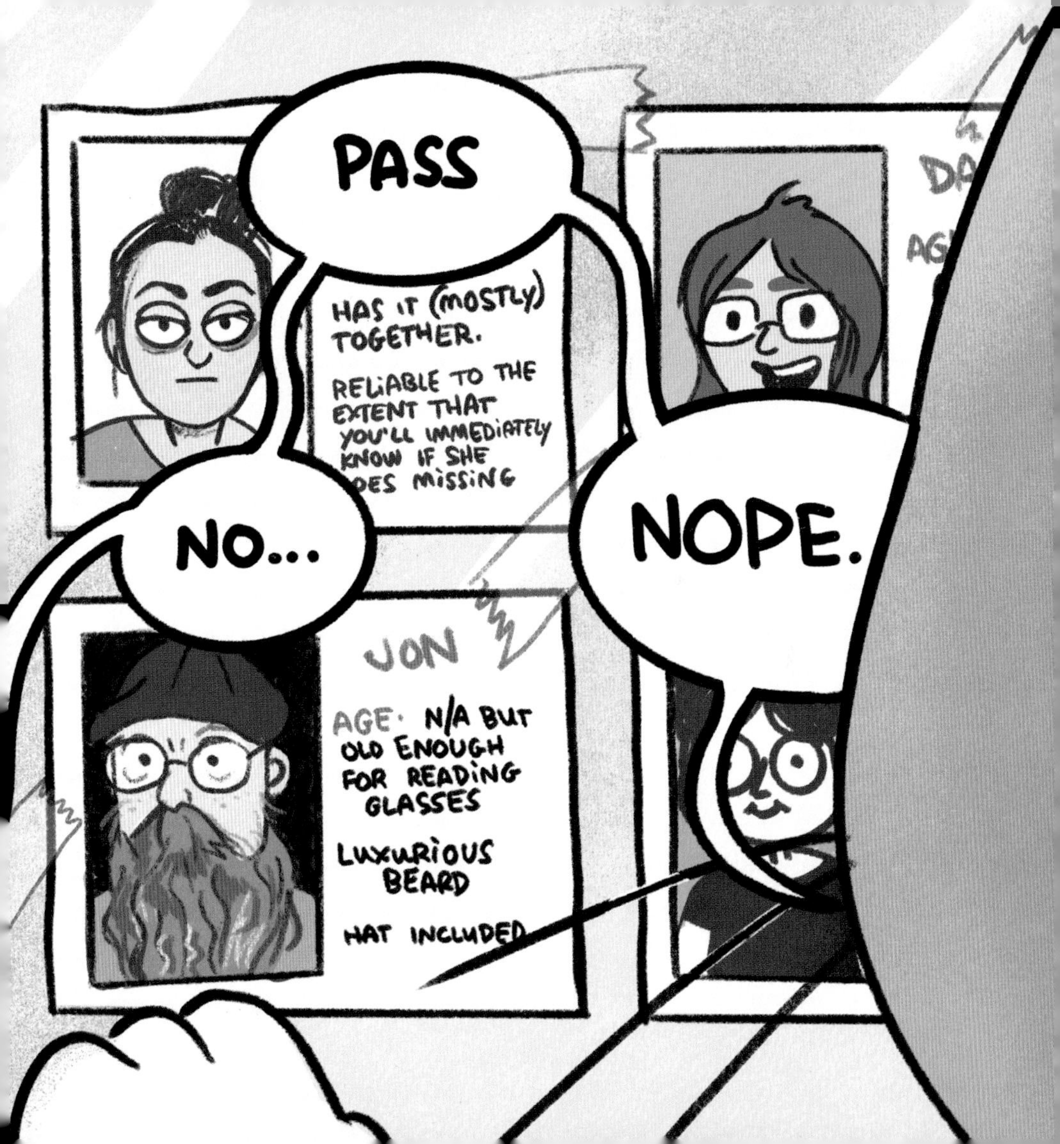
PASS
HAS IT (MOSTLY) TOGETHER.
RELIABLE TO THE EXTENT THAT YOU'LL IMMEDIATELY KNOW IF SHE
OES MISSING
NO...
NOPE.
JON
AGE: N/A BUT OLD ENOUGH FOR READING GLASSES
LUXURIOUS BEARD
HAT INCLUDED

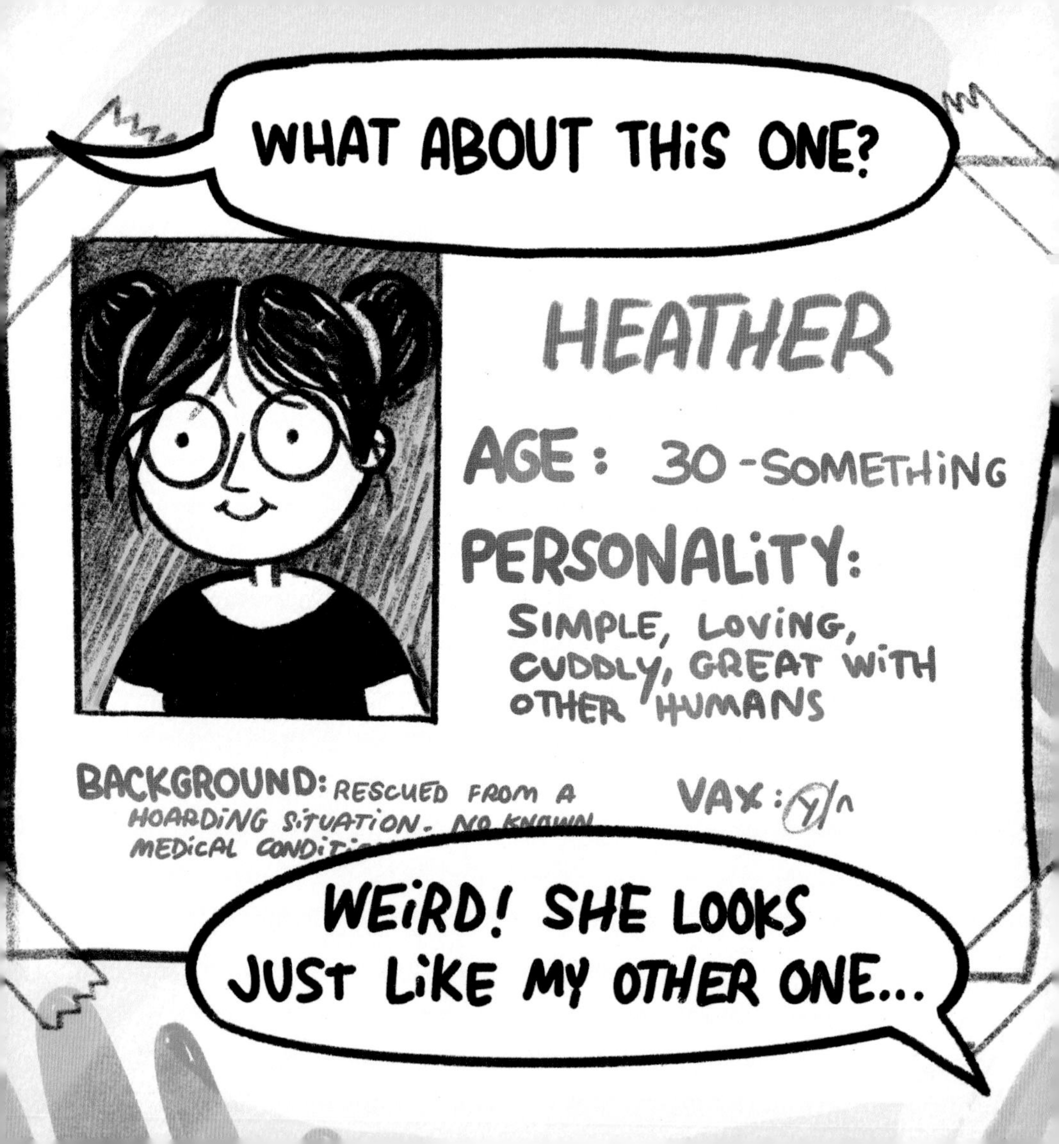
WHAT ABOUT THIS ONE?
HEATHER
AGE: 30-SOMETHING
PERSONALITY:
SIMPLE, LOVING, CUDDLY, GREAT WITH OTHER HUMANS
BACKGROUND: RESCUED FROM A HOARDING SITUATION. NO KNOWN
MEDICAL
VAX: Y/
WEIRD! SHE LOOKS JUST LIKE MY OTHER ONE...

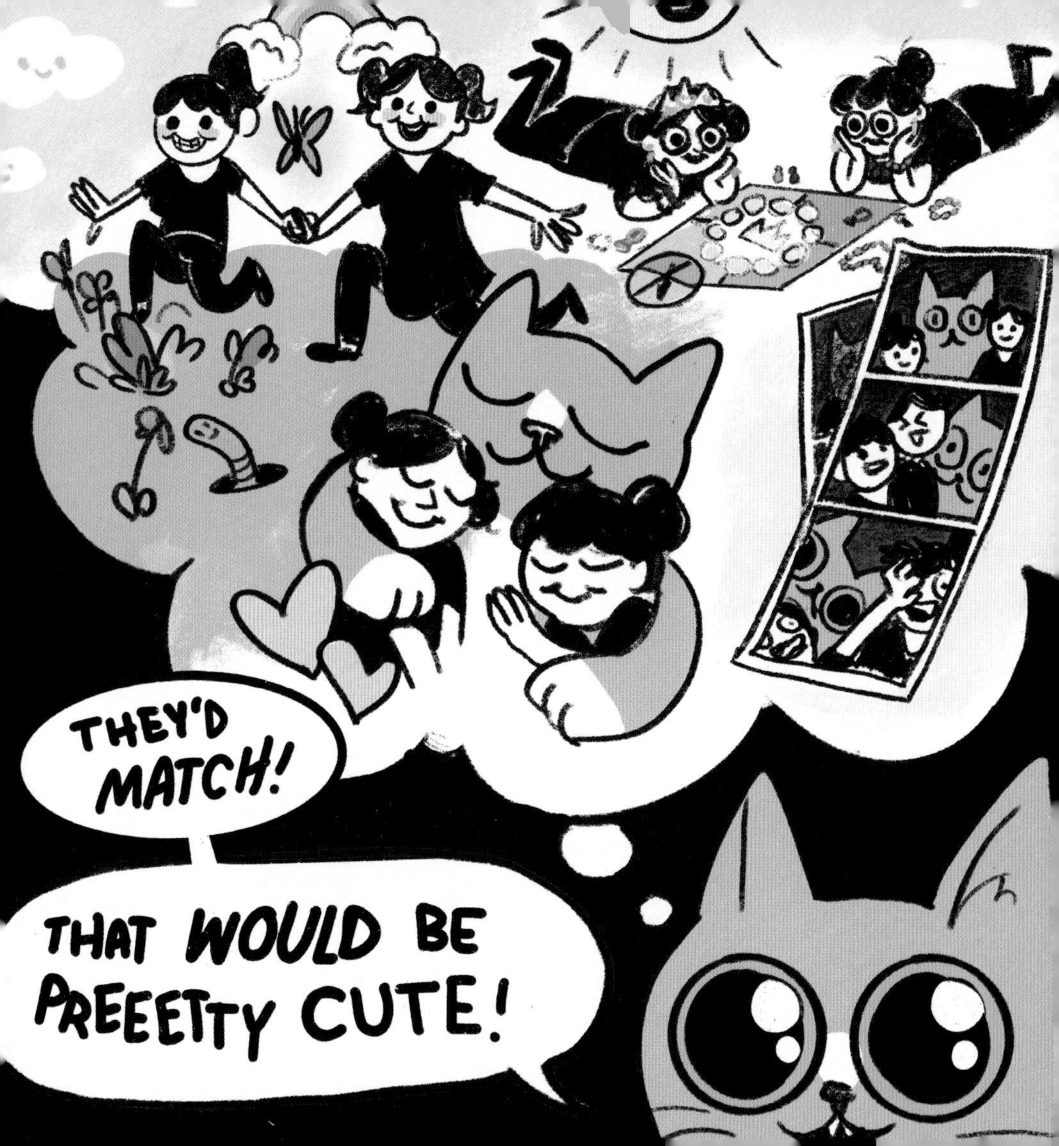
THEY'D MATCH!
THAT WOULD BE PREEETTY CUTE!

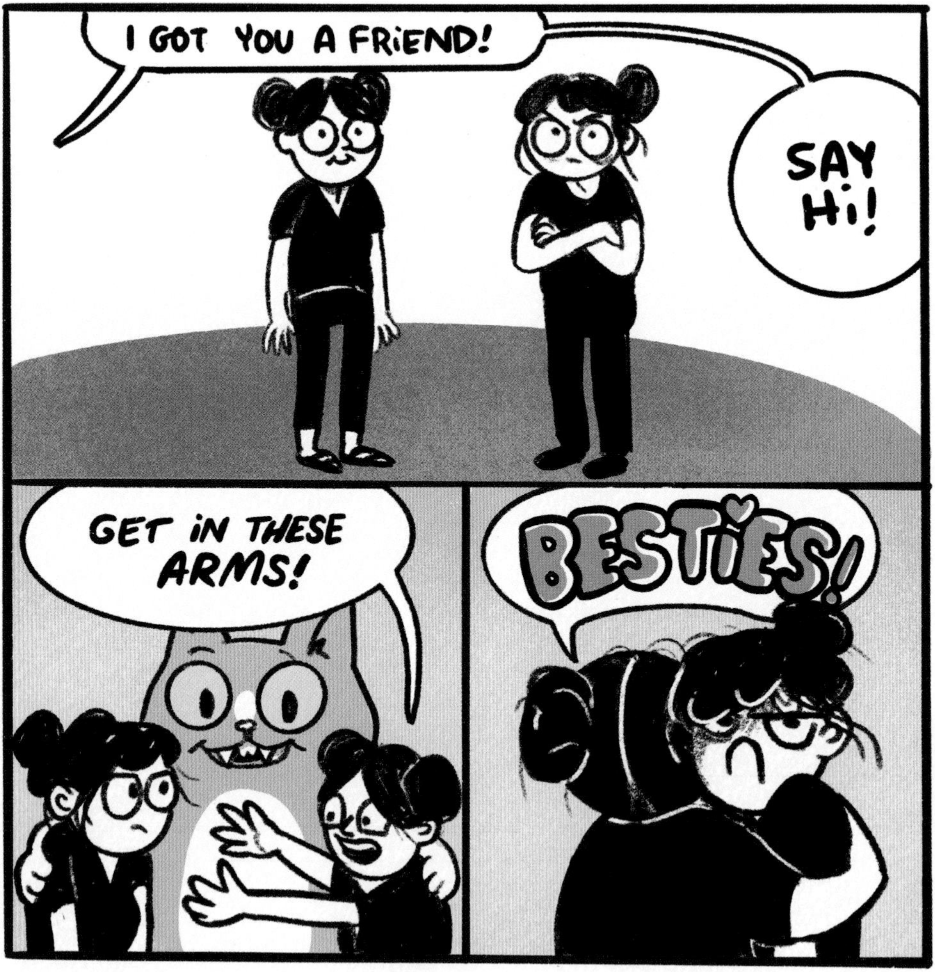
I GOT YOU A FRiEND!
SAY Hi!
GET iN THESE ARMS!
BESTiES!

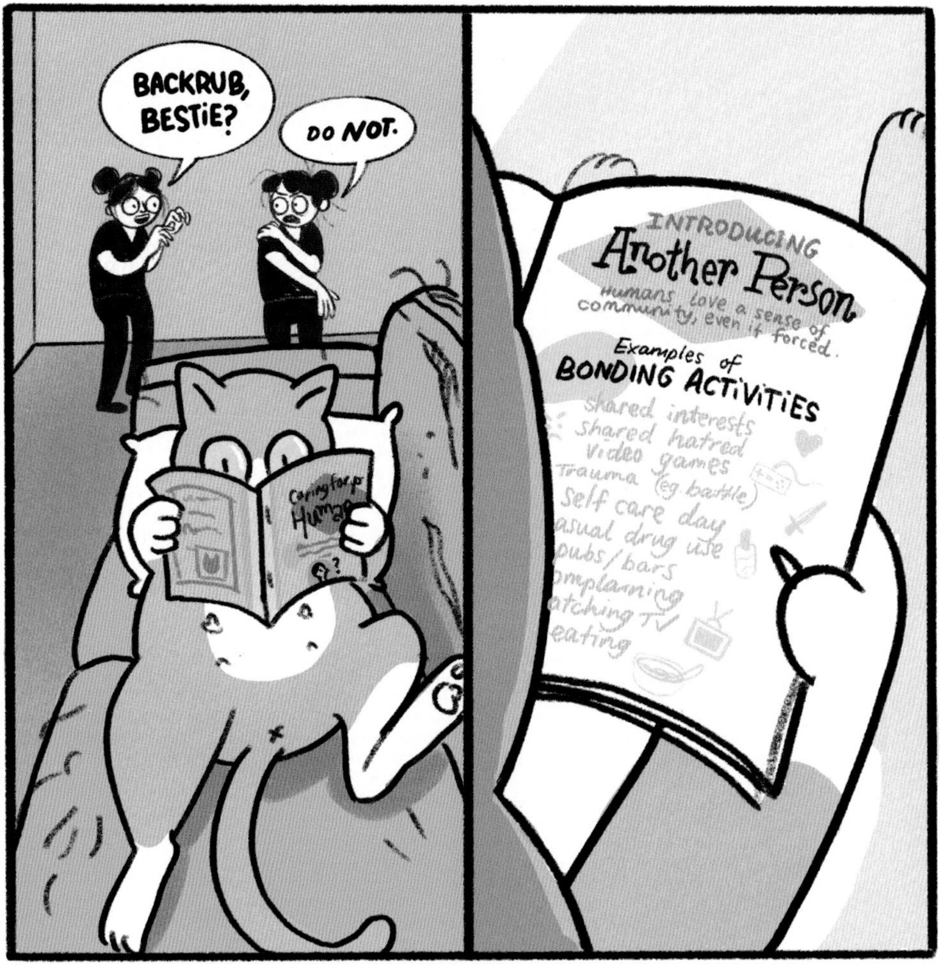
BACKRUB, BESTiE?
DO NOT.
INTRODUCING
Another Person
Humans love a sense of community, even if forced.
Examples of
BONDING ACTiViTiES
shared interests
shared hatred
video games
Trauma (eg. battle)
self care day
asual drug use
pubs/bars
omplaining
atching TV
eating

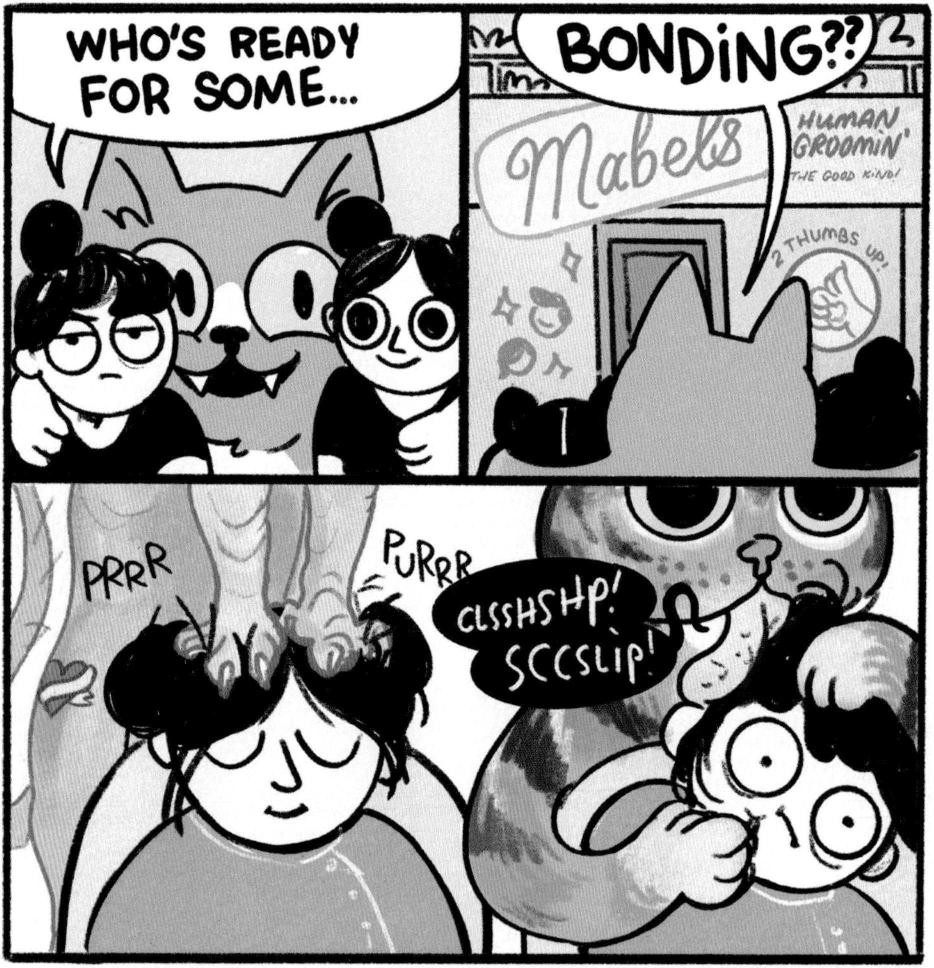
WHO'S READY FOR SOME...
BONDING??
Mabel's
HUMAN GROOMIN'
THE GOOD KIND!
2 THUMBS UP!
PRRR
PURRR
CLSSHSHP! SCCSLIP!

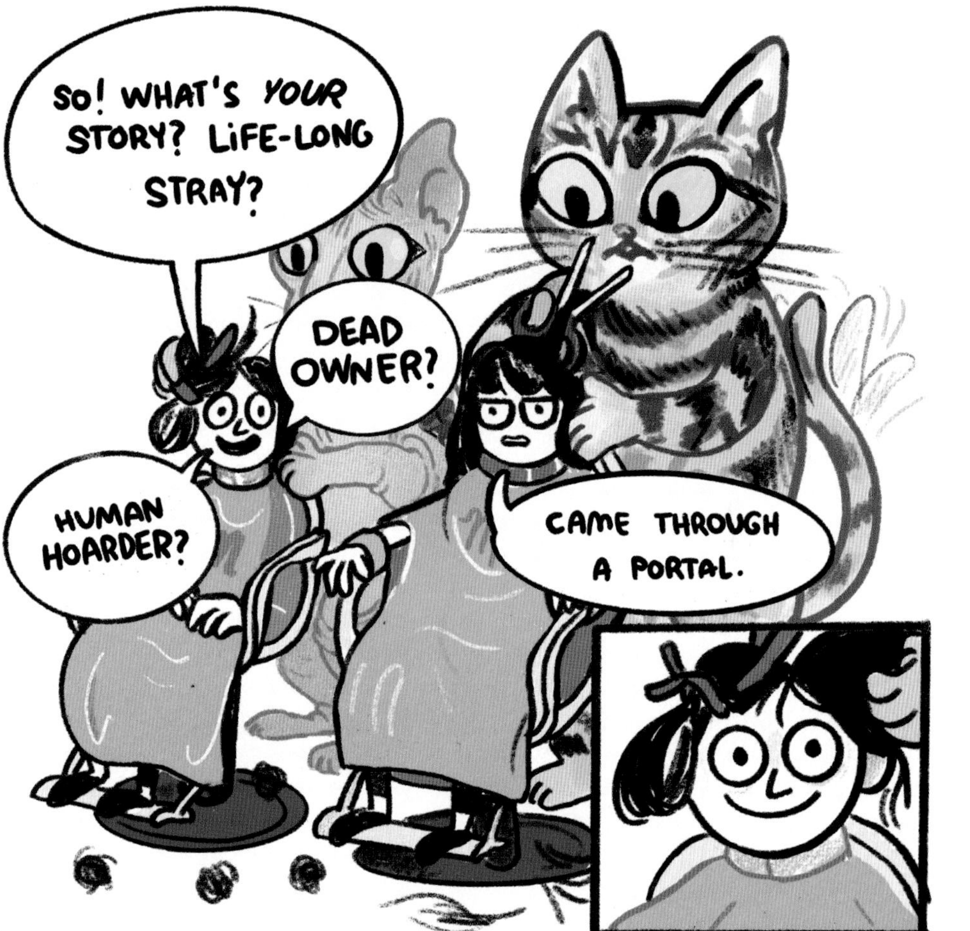
SO! WHAT'S YOUR STORY? LIFE-LONG STRAY?
DEAD OWNER?
HUMAN HOARDER?
CAME THROUGH A PORTAL.

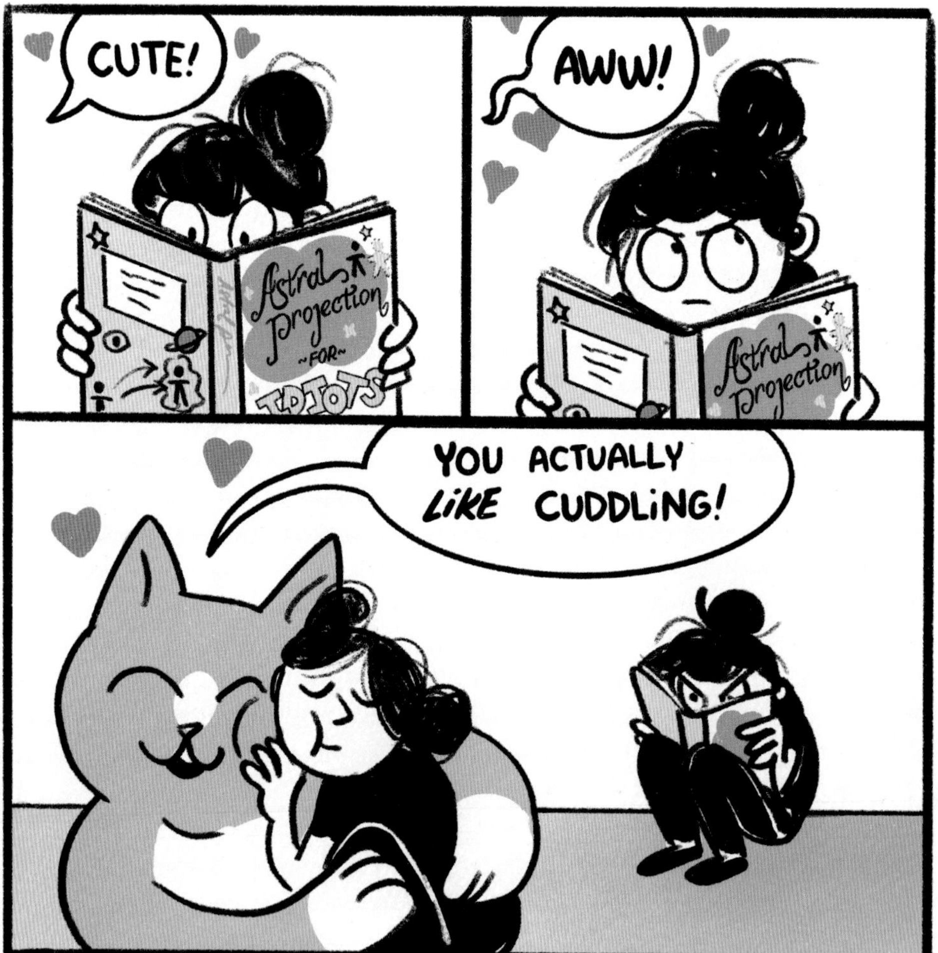
CUTE!
Astral Projection ~FOR~ IDIOTS
AWW!
Astral Projection
YOU ACTUALLY LIKE CUDDLING!

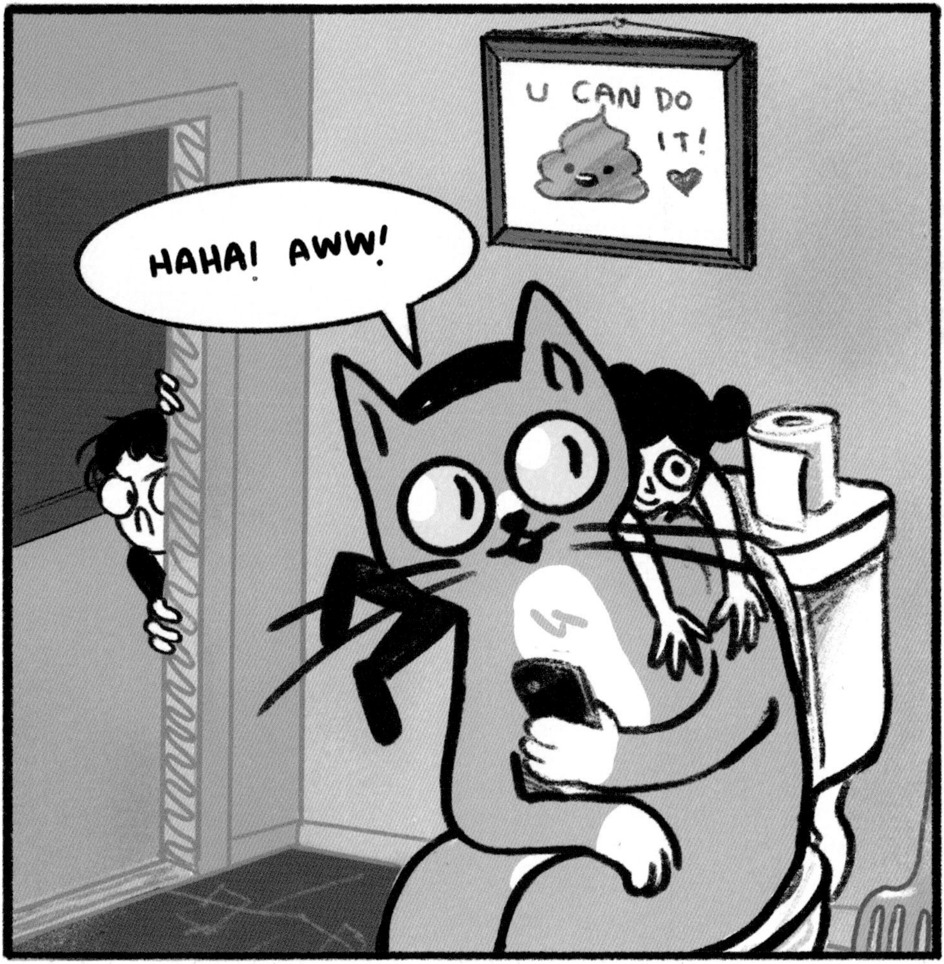
U CAN DO IT!
HAHA! AWW!

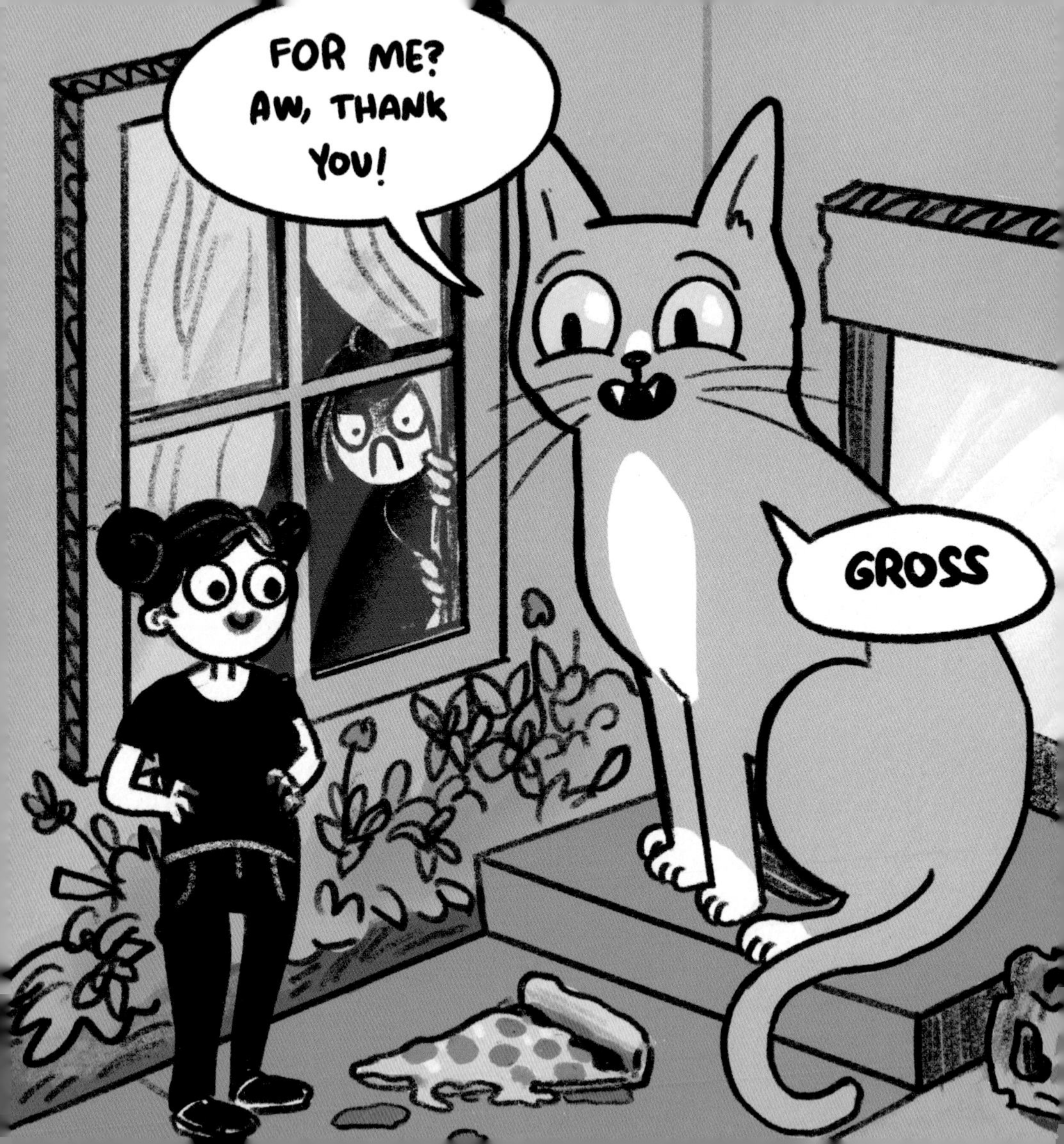
FOR ME? AW, THANK YOU!
GROSS

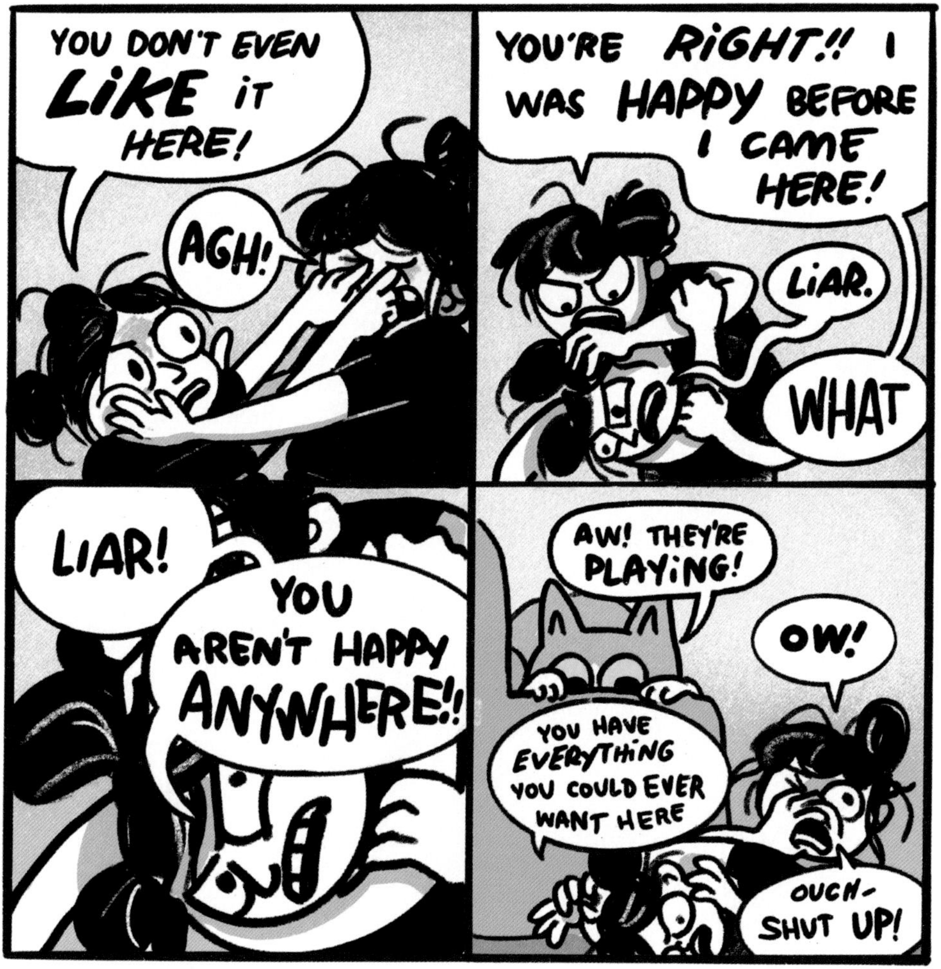
YOU DON'T EVEN LIKE IT HERE!
AGH!
YOU'RE RIGHT!! I WAS HAPPY BEFORE I CAME HERE!
LIAR.
WHAT
LIAR!
YOU AREN'T HAPPY ANYWHERE!!
AW! THEY'RE PLAYING!
OW!
YOU HAVE EVERYTHING YOU COULD EVER WANT HERE
OUCH- SHUT UP!

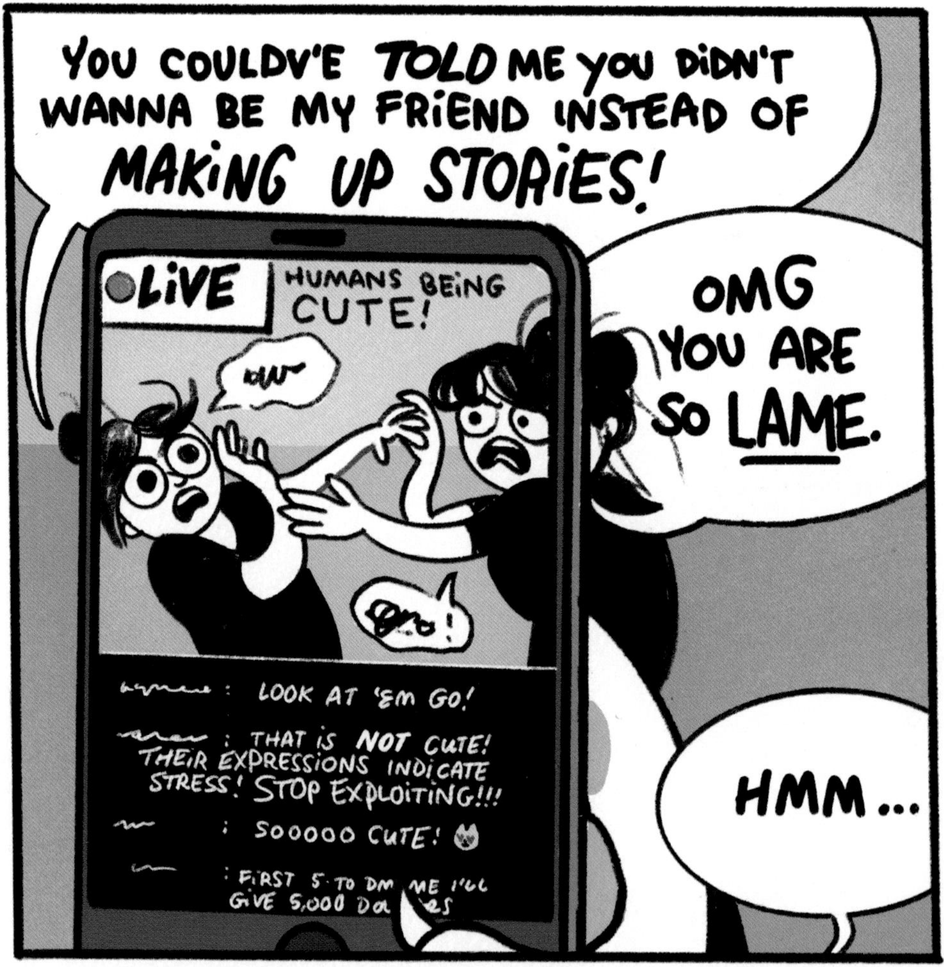
YOU COULDV'E TOLD ME YOU DIDN'T WANNA BE MY FRIEND INSTEAD OF MAKING UP STORIES!
LIVE
HUMANS BEING CUTE!
LOOK AT 'EM GO!
THAT IS NOT CUTE! THEIR EXPRESSIONS INDICATE STRESS! STOP EXPLOITING!!!
SOOOOO CUTE!
FIRST 5 TO DM ME I'LL GIVE 5,000
OMG YOU ARE SO LAME.
HMM...

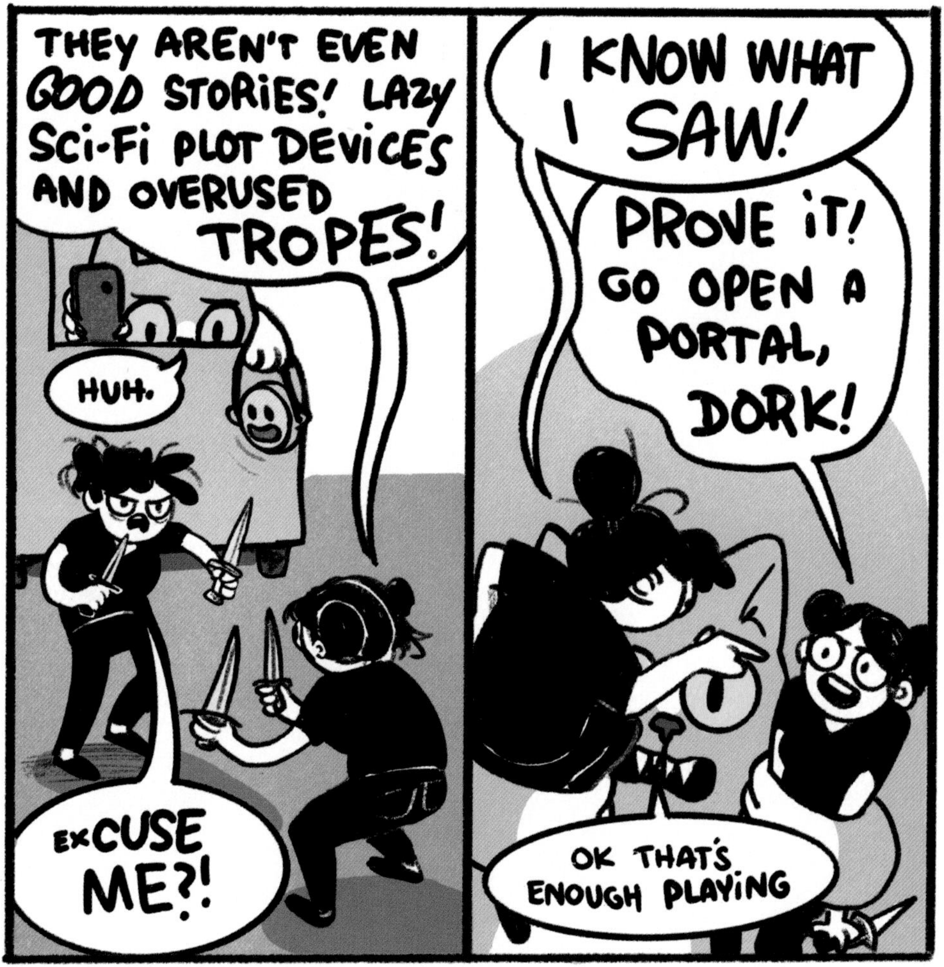
THEY AREN'T EVEN GOOD STORIES! LAZY SCI-FI PLOT DEVICES AND OVERUSED TROPES!
HUH.
EXCUSE ME?!
I KNOW WHAT I SAW!
PROVE IT! GO OPEN A PORTAL, DORK!
OK THAT'S ENOUGH PLAYING

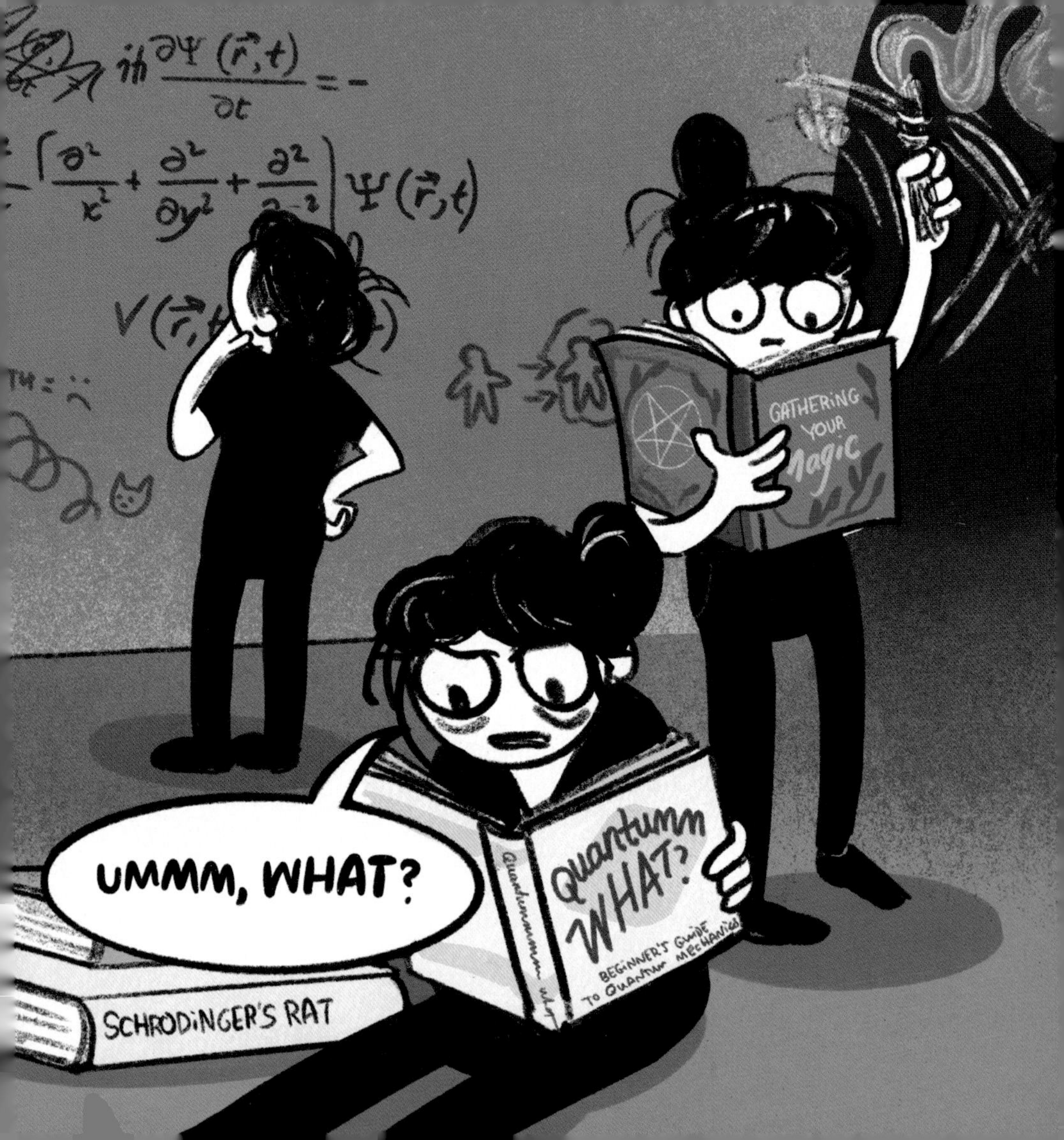
UMMM, WHAT?
GATHERING YOUR Magic
Quantumm WHAT?
BEGINNER'S GUIDE TO QUANTUM MECHANICS
SCHRODINGER'S RAT

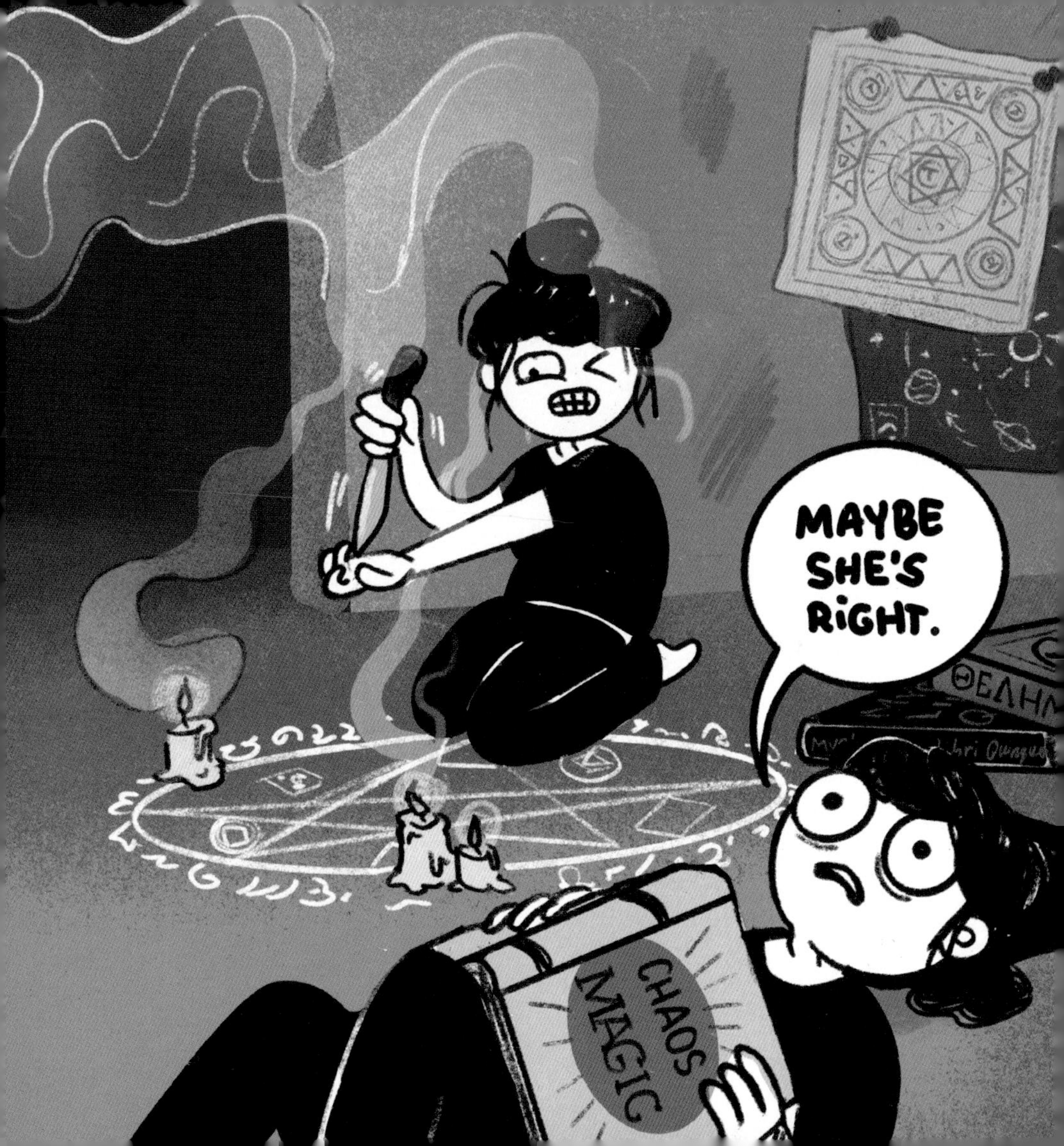
MAYBE SHE'S RIGHT.
CHAOS MAGIC

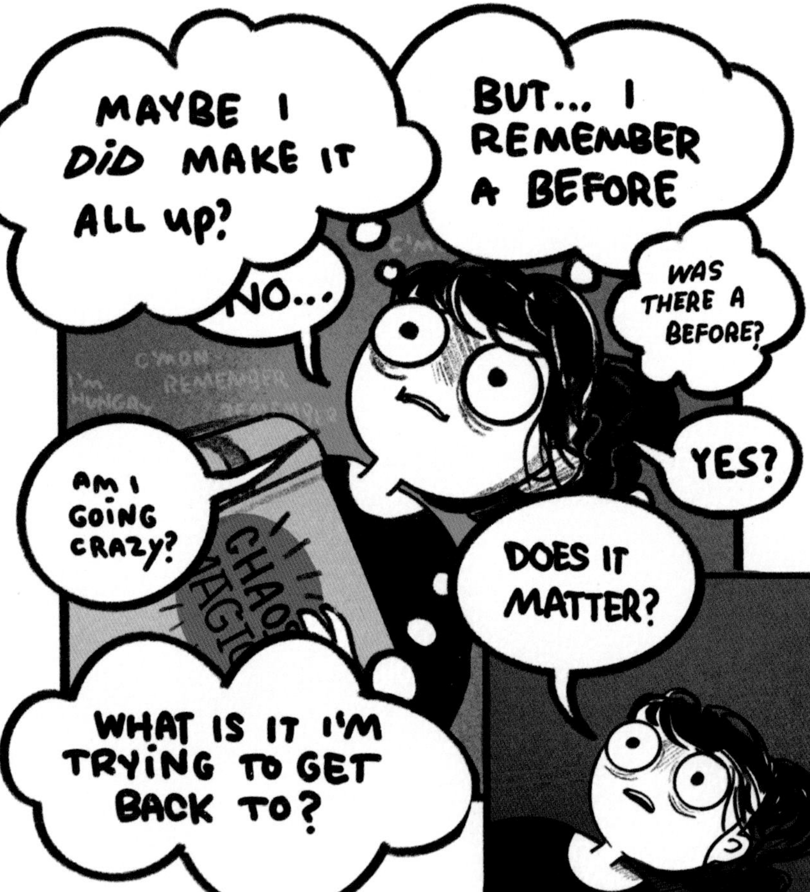
MAYBE I DID MAKE IT ALL UP?
NO...
BUT... I REMEMBER A BEFORE
WAS THERE A BEFORE?
AM I GOING CRAZY?
YES?
DOES IT MATTER?
WHAT IS IT I'M TRYING TO GET BACK TO?

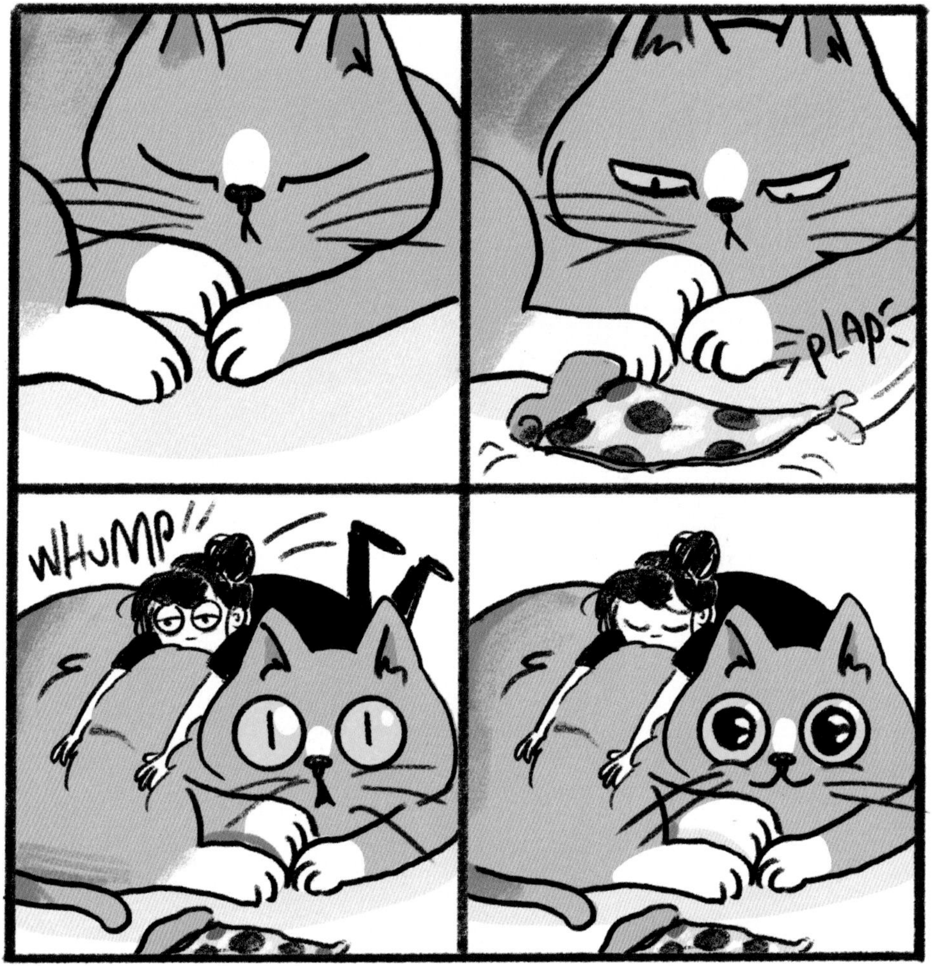
PLAP
WHUMP

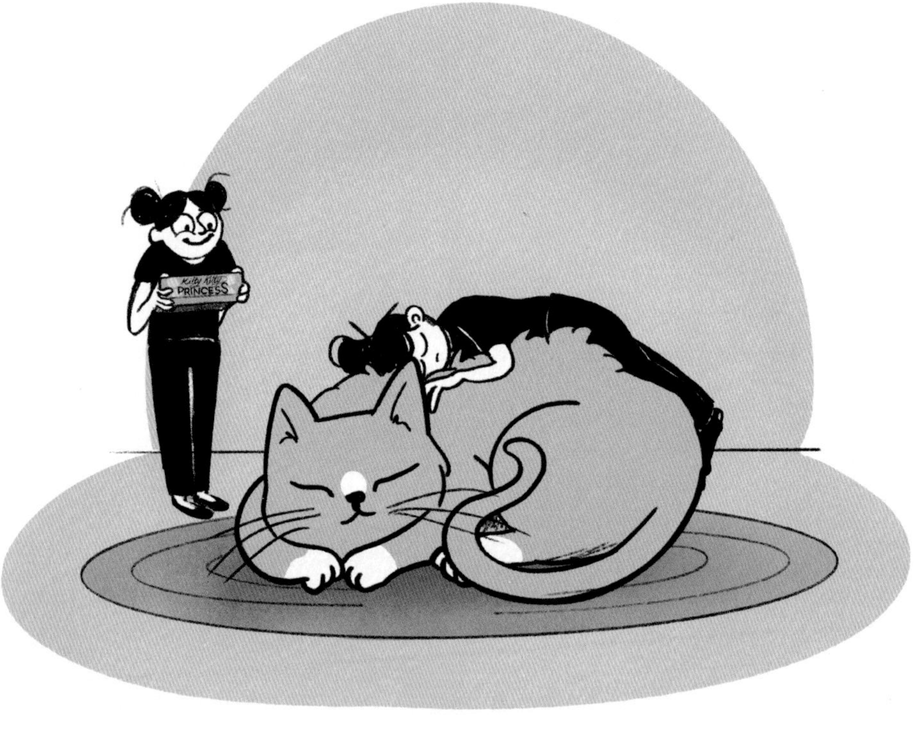
PRINCESS

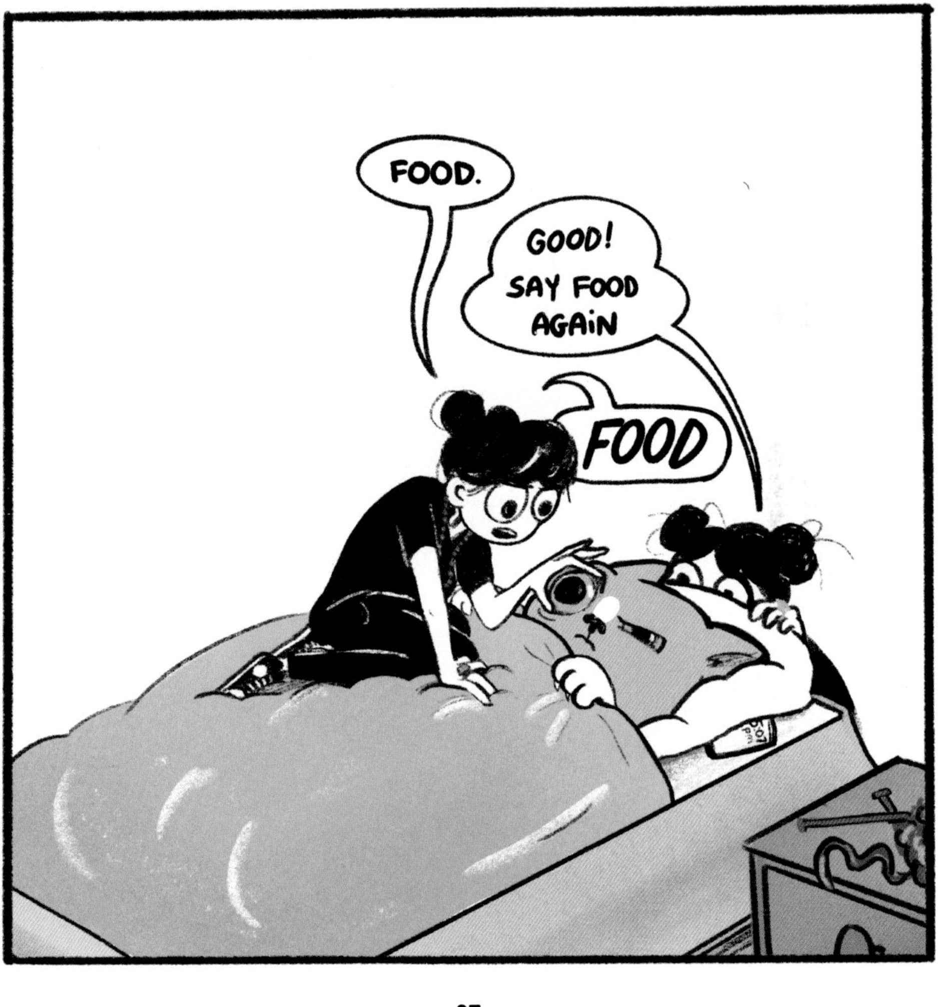
FOOD.
GOOD! SAY FOOD AGAIN
FOOD

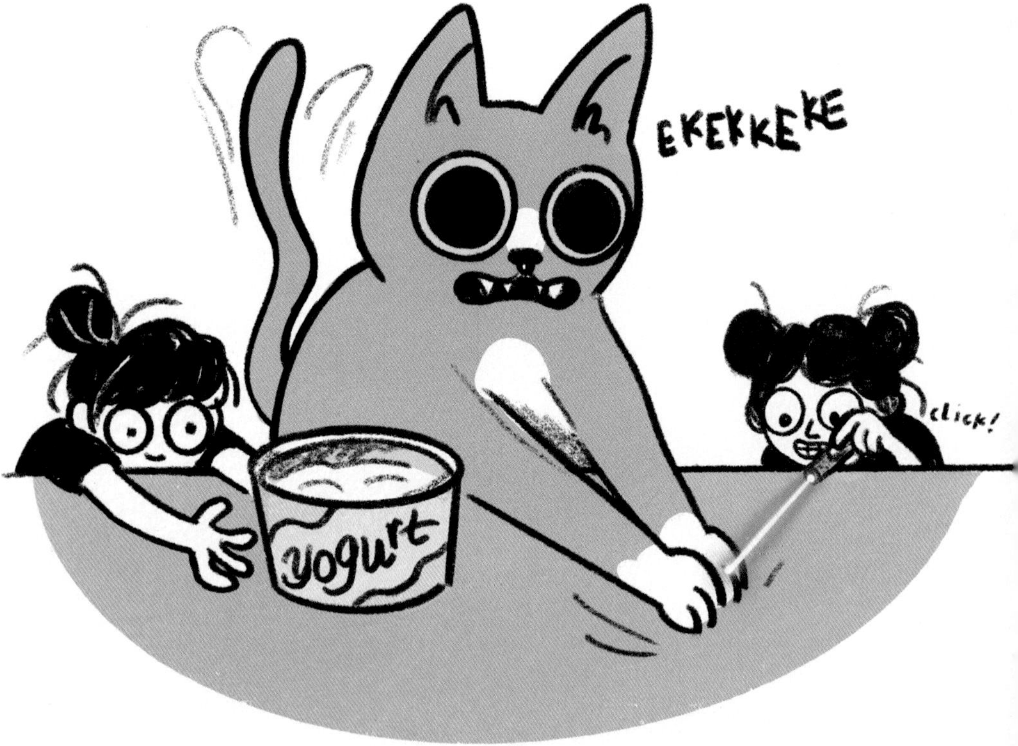
EKEKKEKE
click!
yogurt

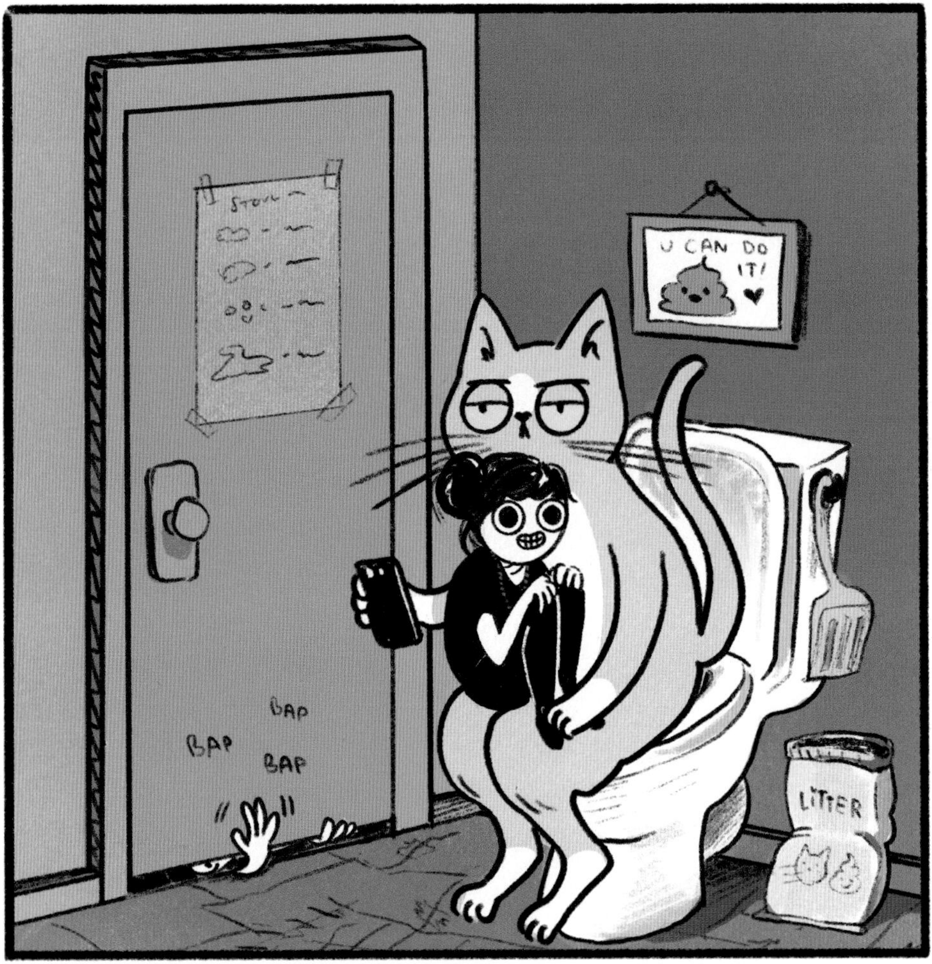
U CAN DO IT!
BAP
BAP
BAP
LITTER

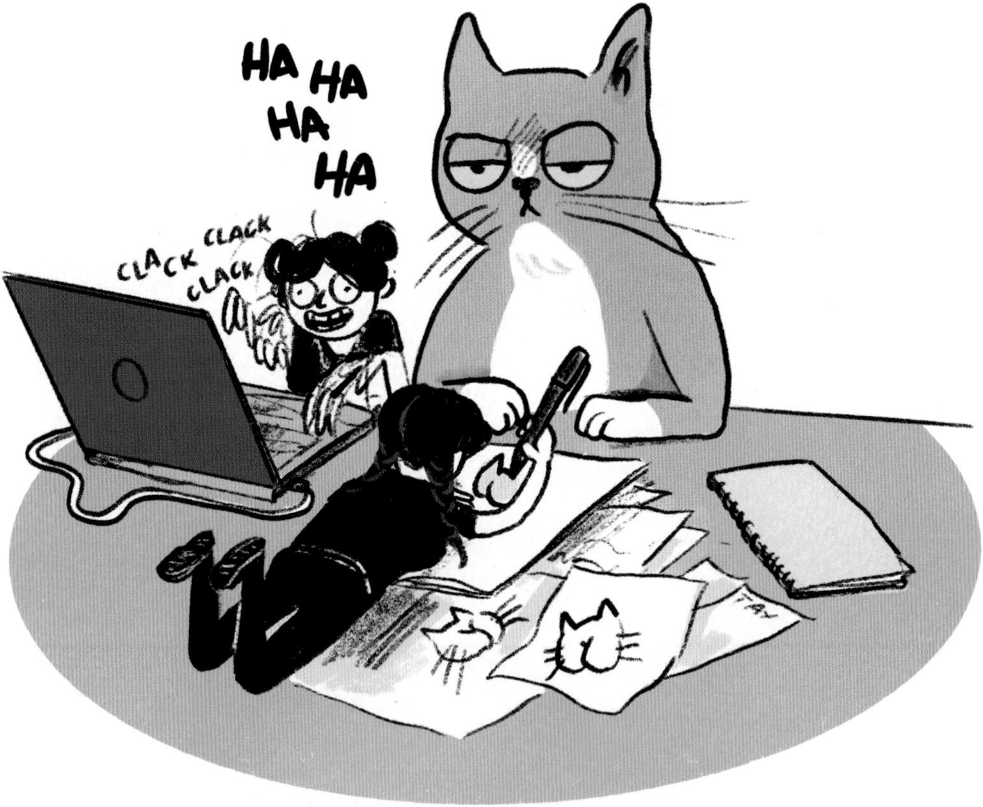
HA HA
HA
HA
CLACK CLACK
CLACK

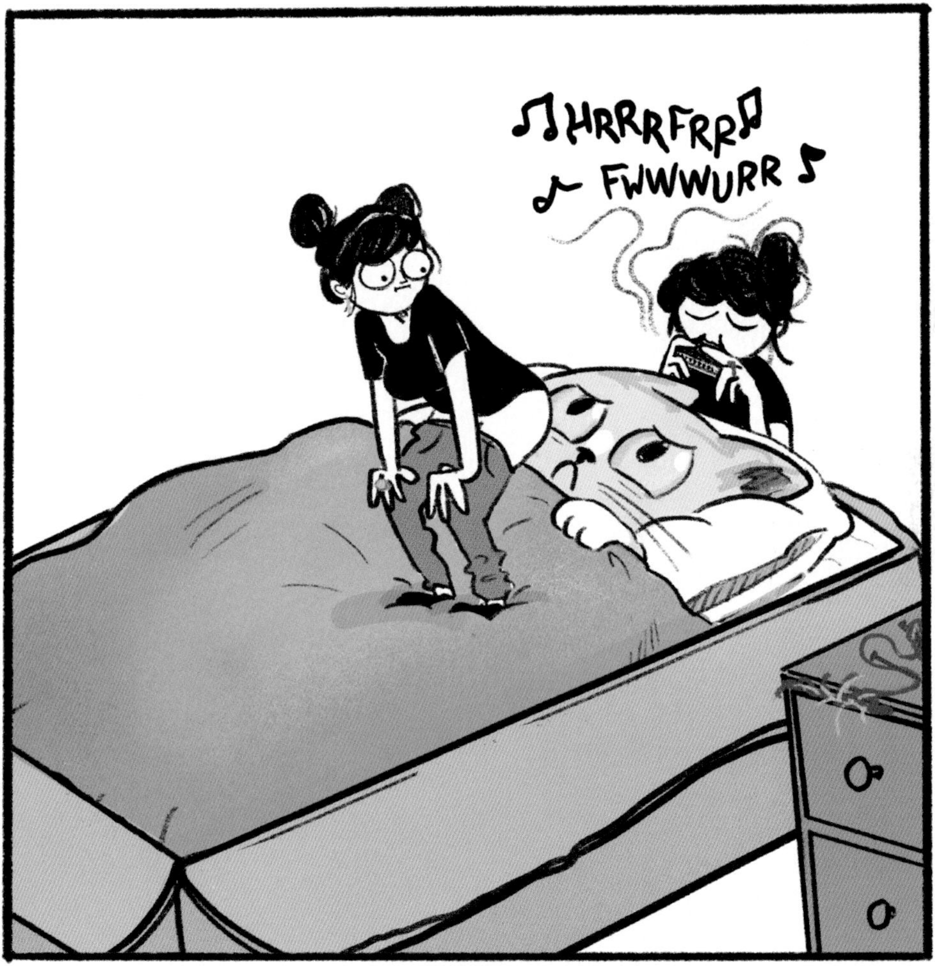
HRRRFRR
FWWWURR

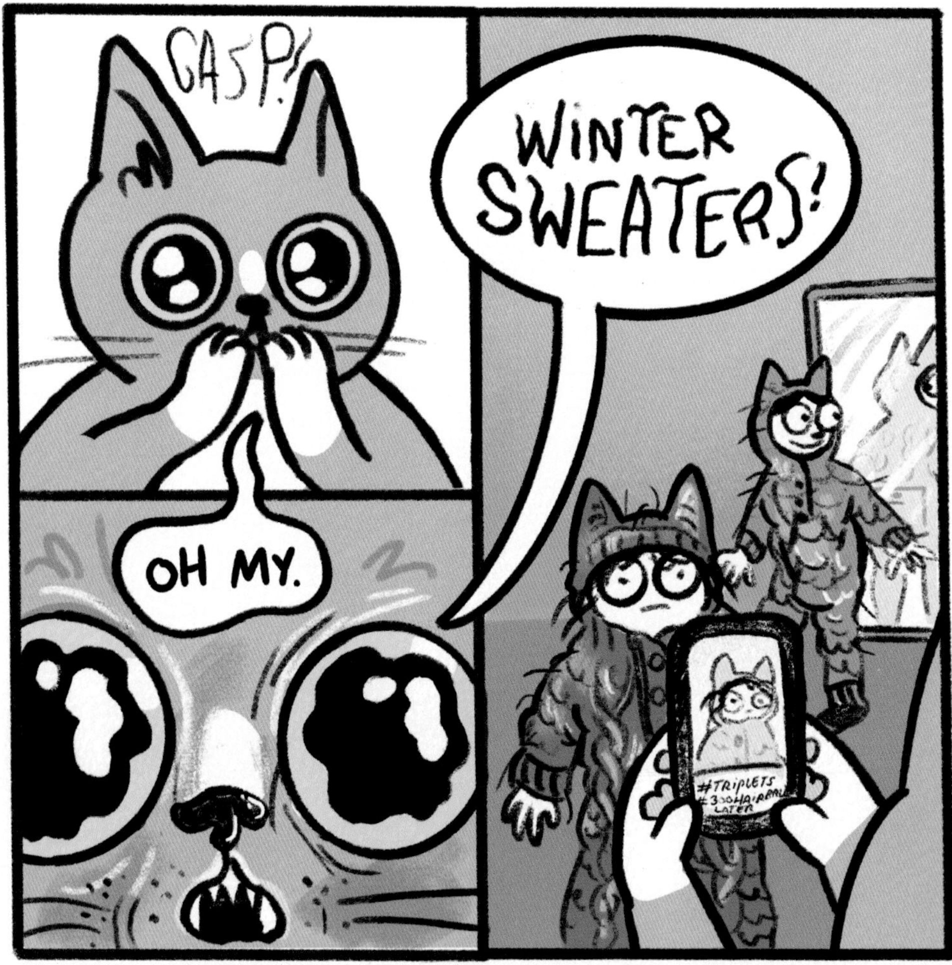
GASP!
OH MY.
WINTER SWEATERS!
#TRIPLETS

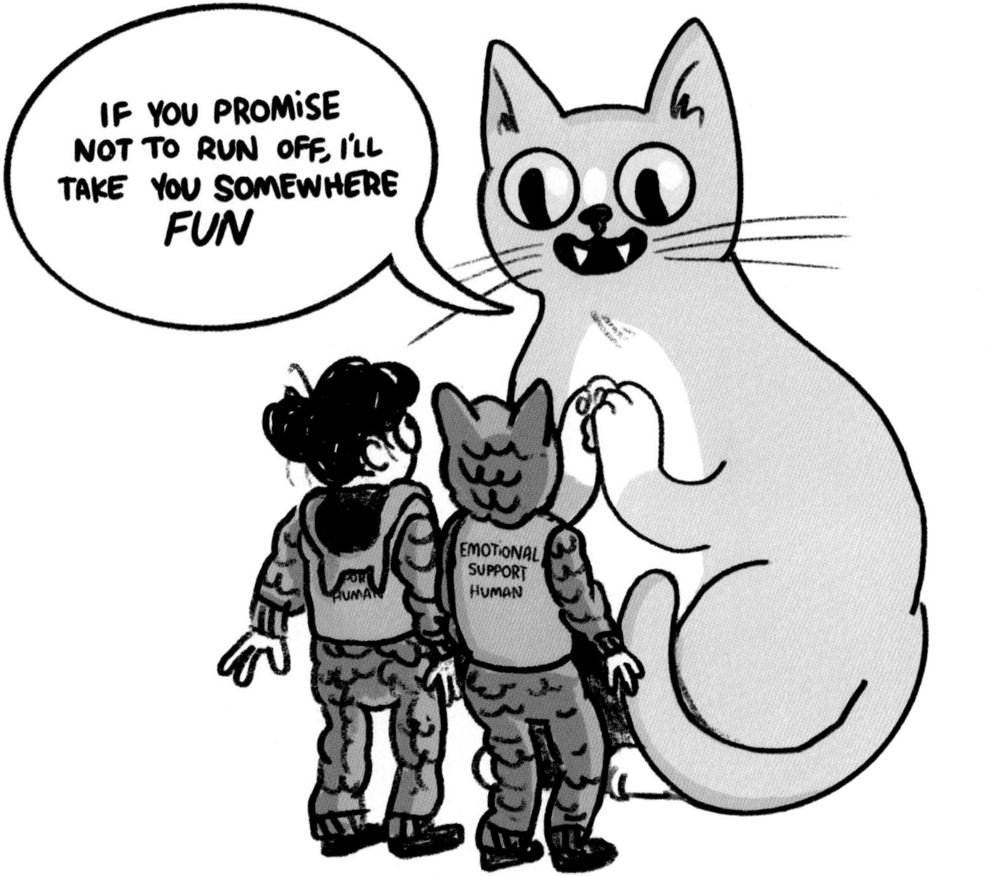
IF YOU PROMISE NOT TO RUN OFF, I'LL TAKE YOU SOMEWHERE *FUN*
EMOTIONAL SUPPORT HUMAN

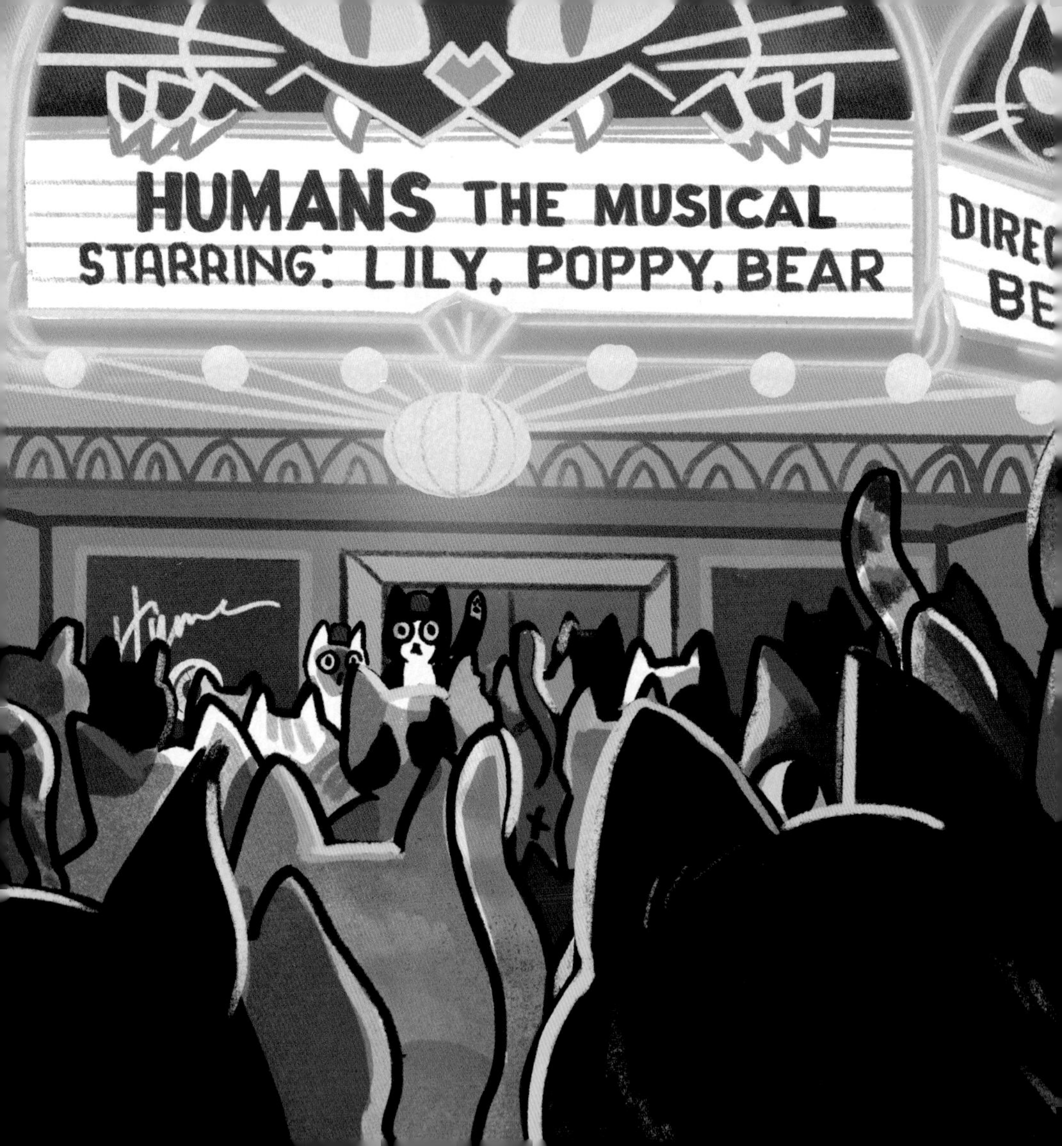
HUMANS THE MUSICAL
STARRING: LILY, POPPY, BEAR
DIREC
BE

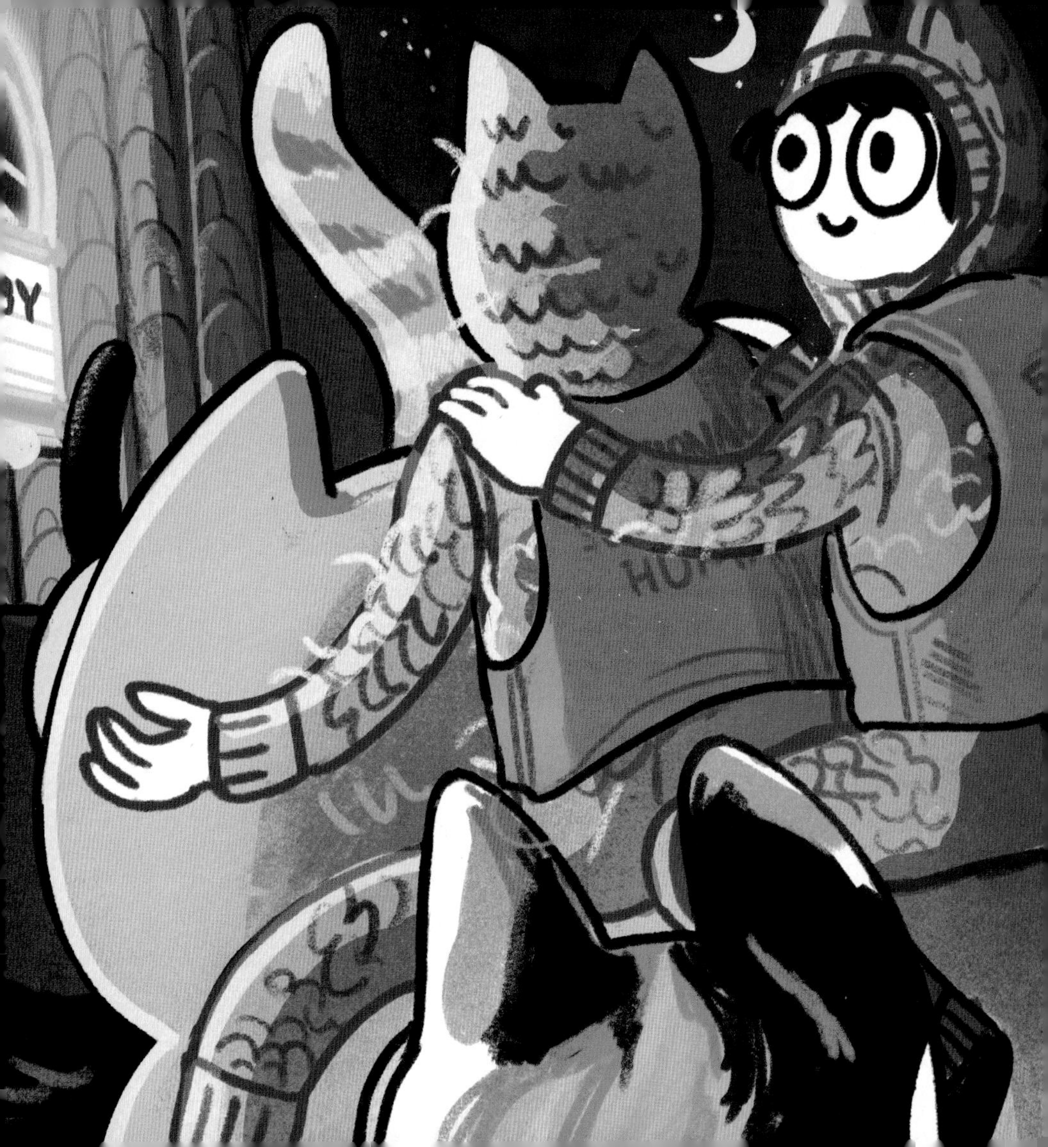

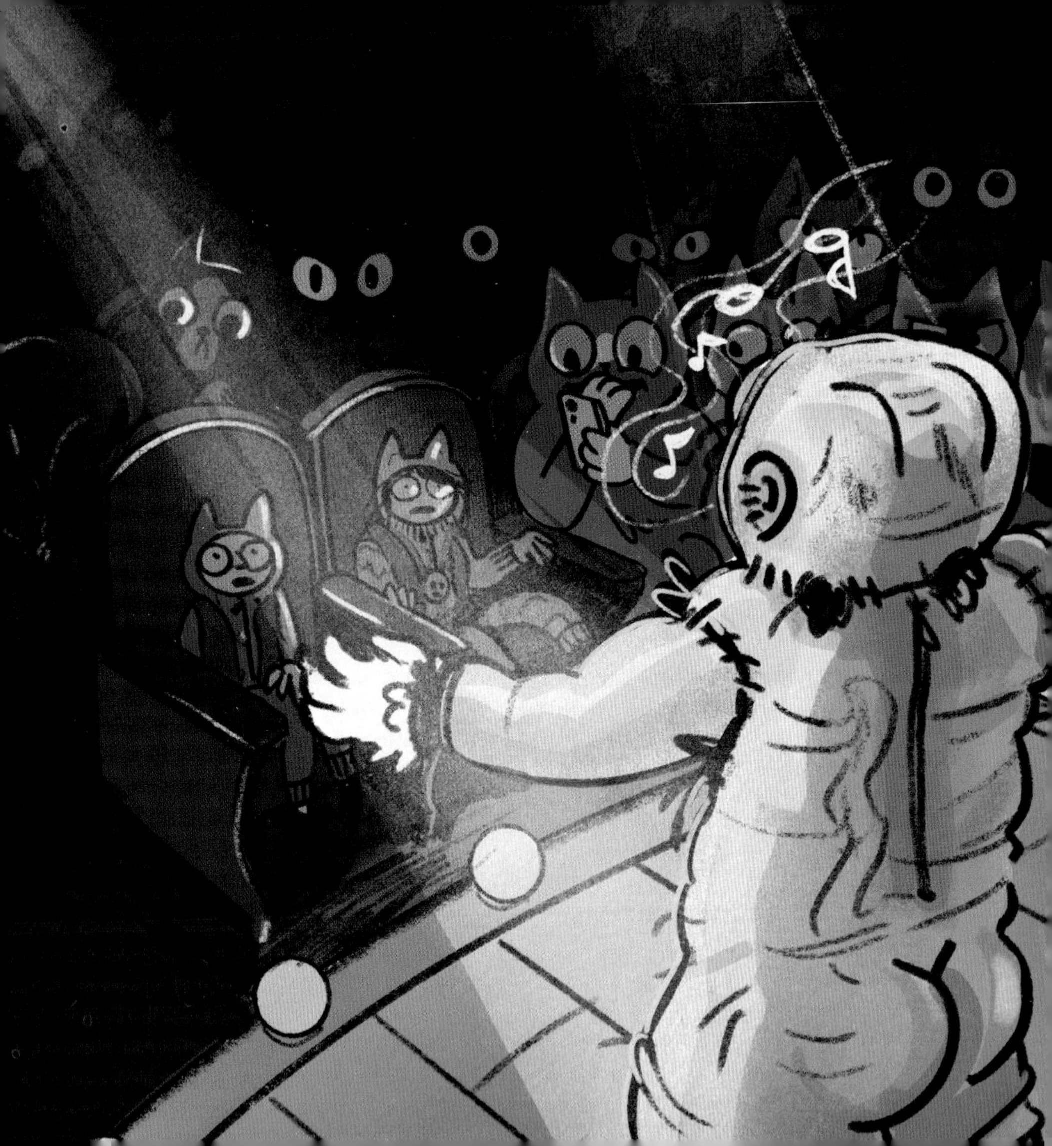

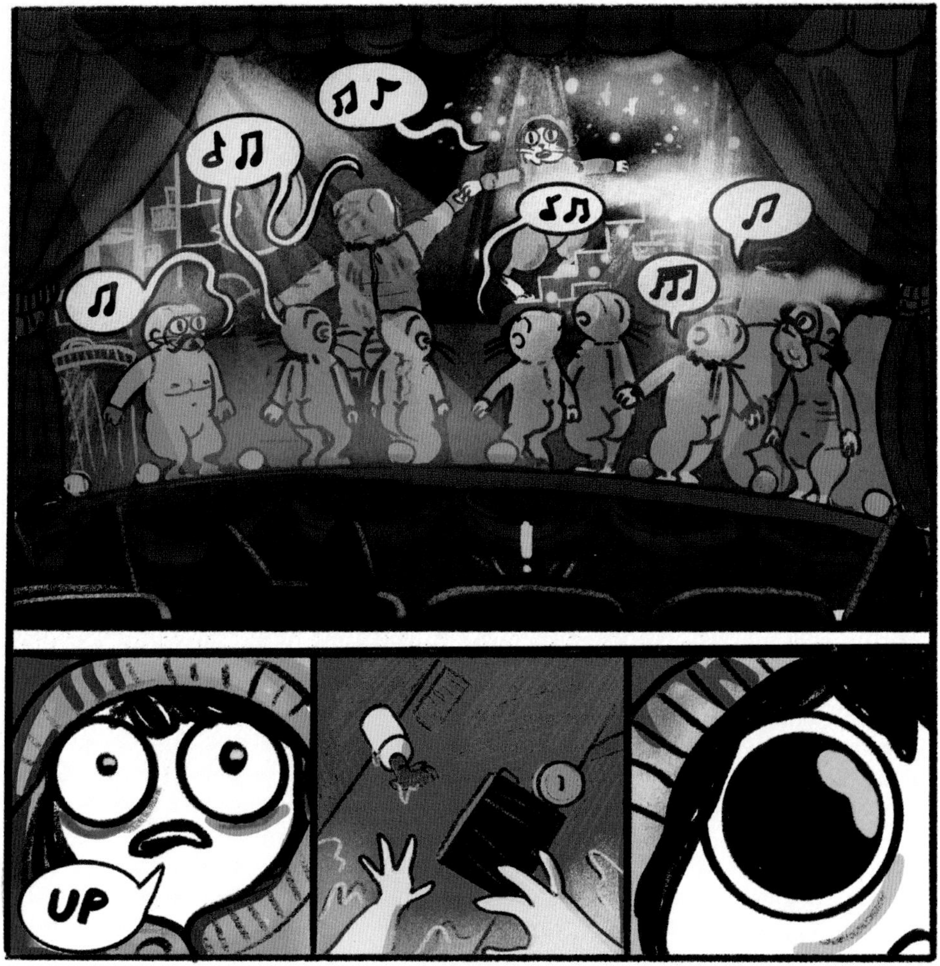
UP

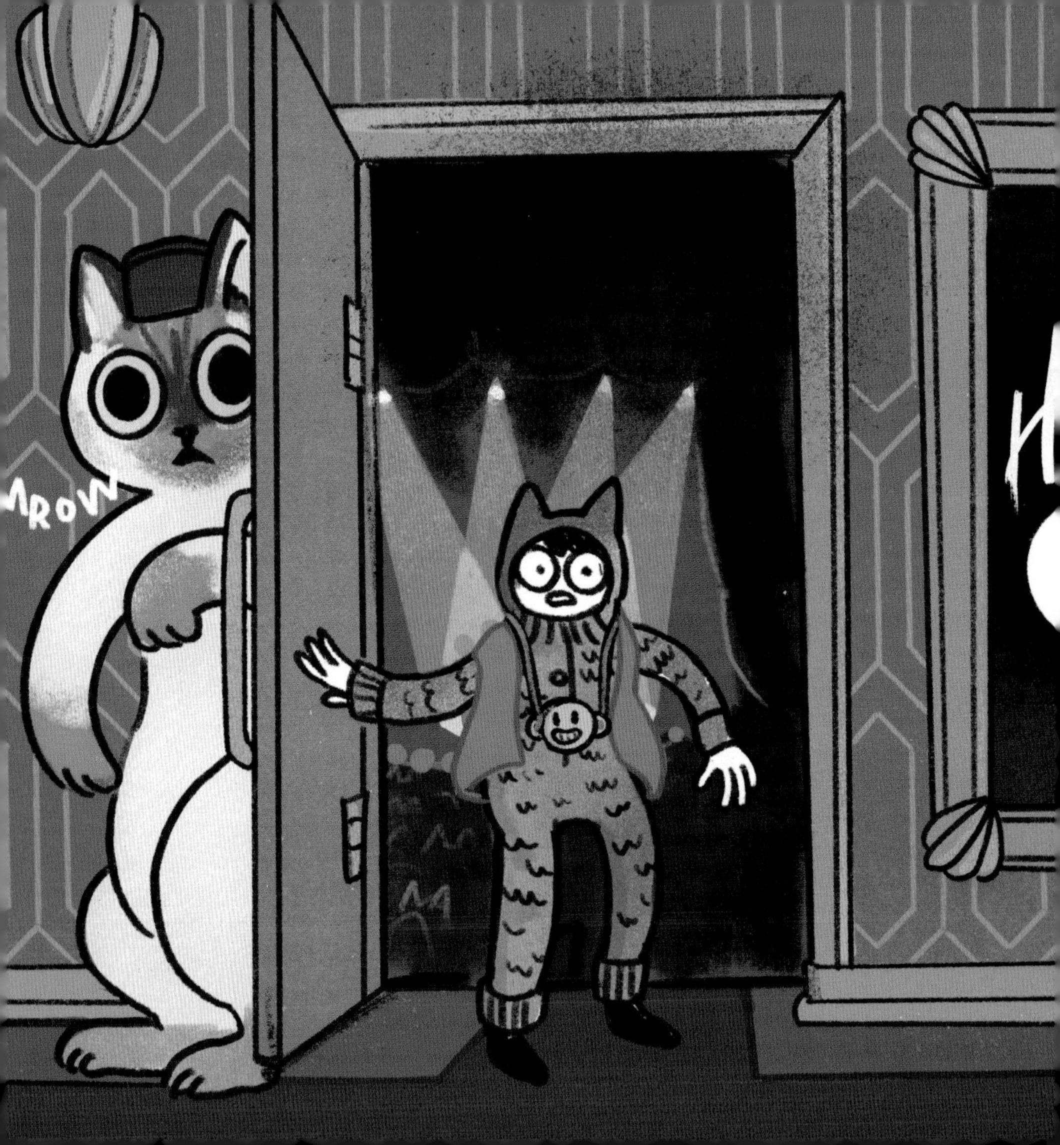
ROW

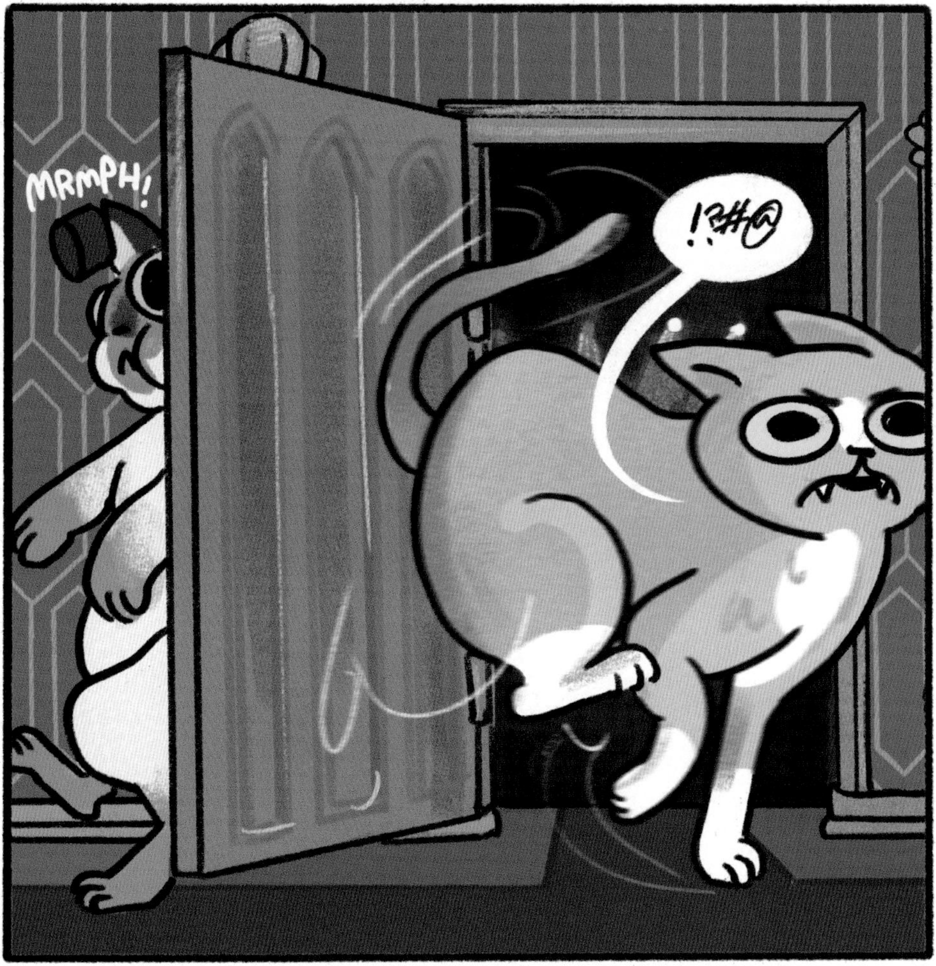
MRMPH!
!?#@

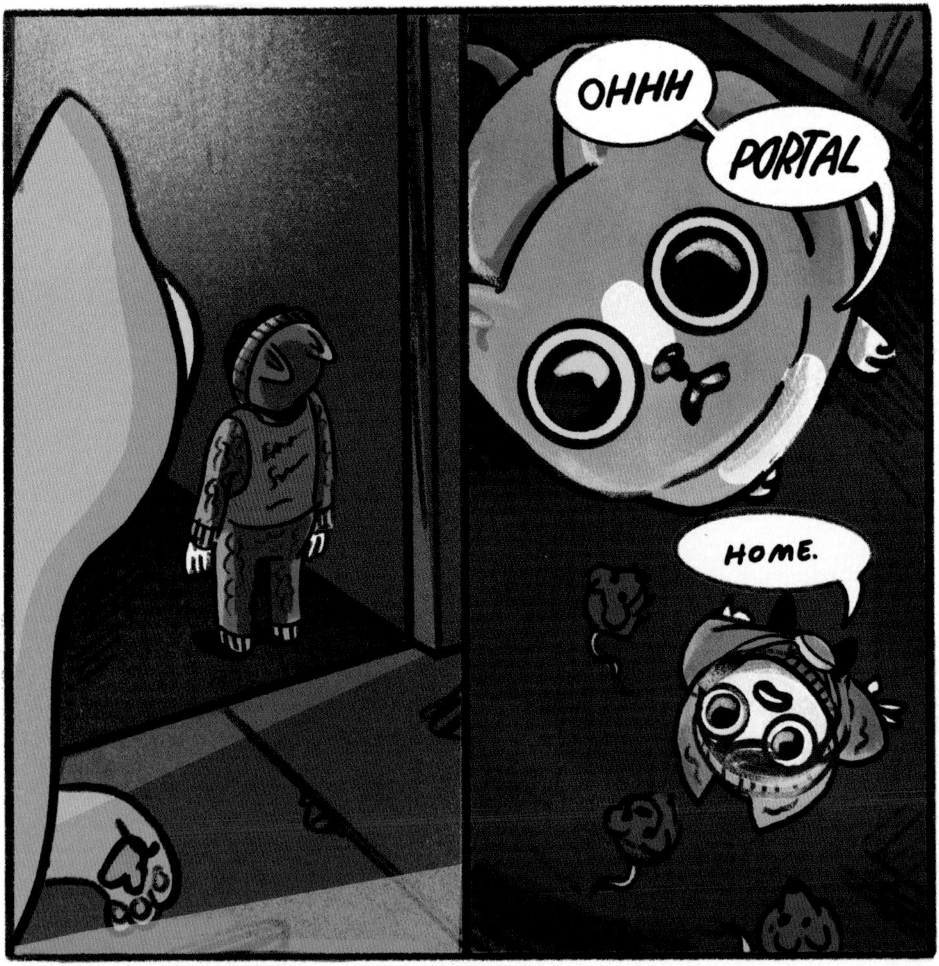
OHHH
PORTAL
HOME.

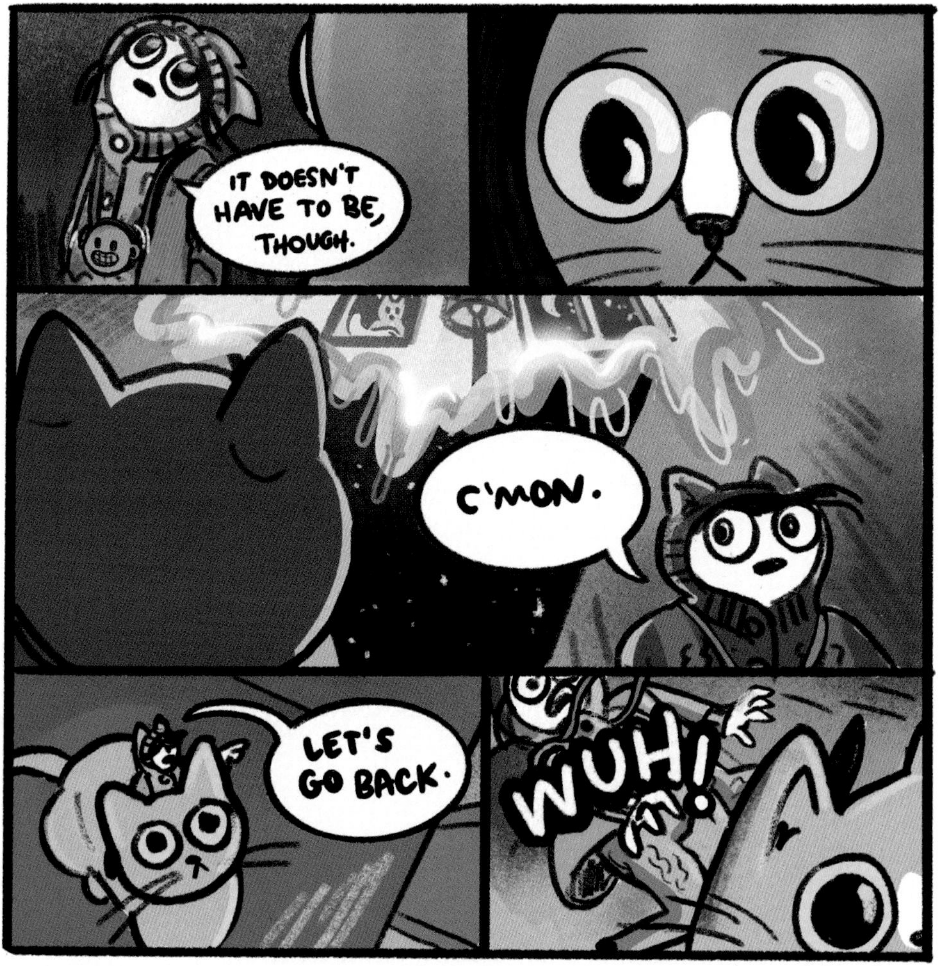
IT DOESN'T HAVE TO BE, THOUGH.
C'MON.
LET'S GO BACK.
WUH!

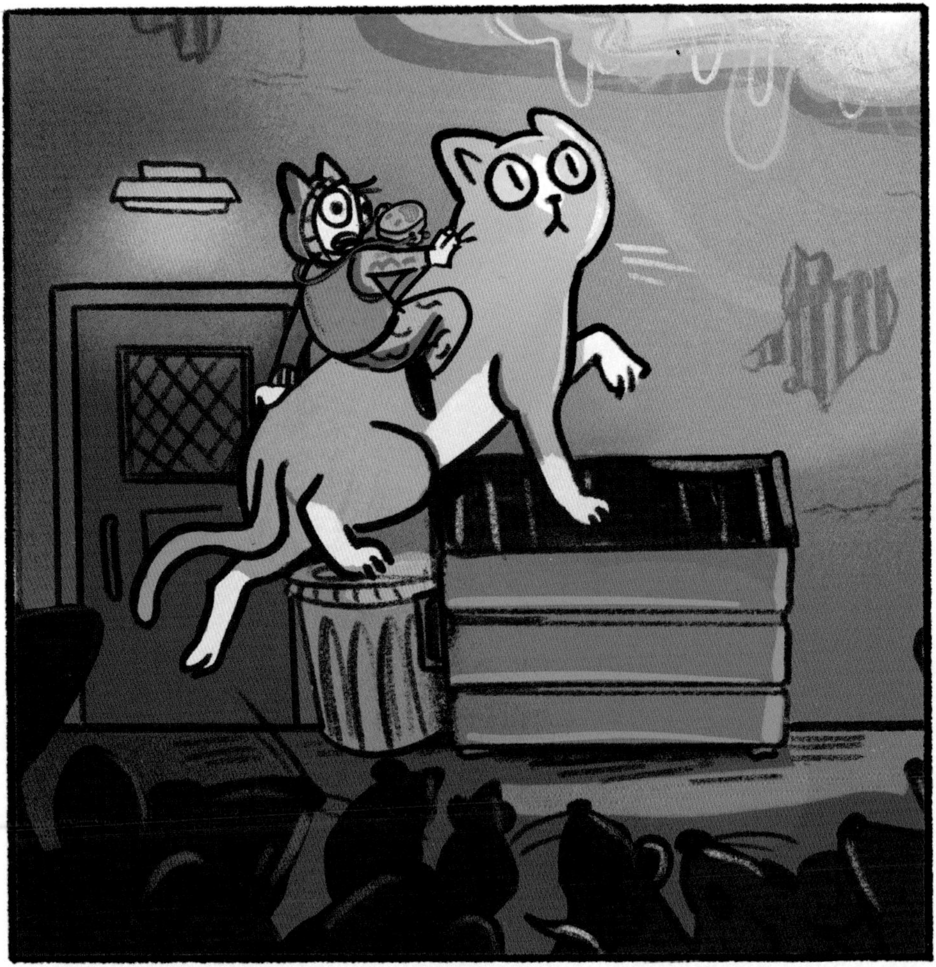

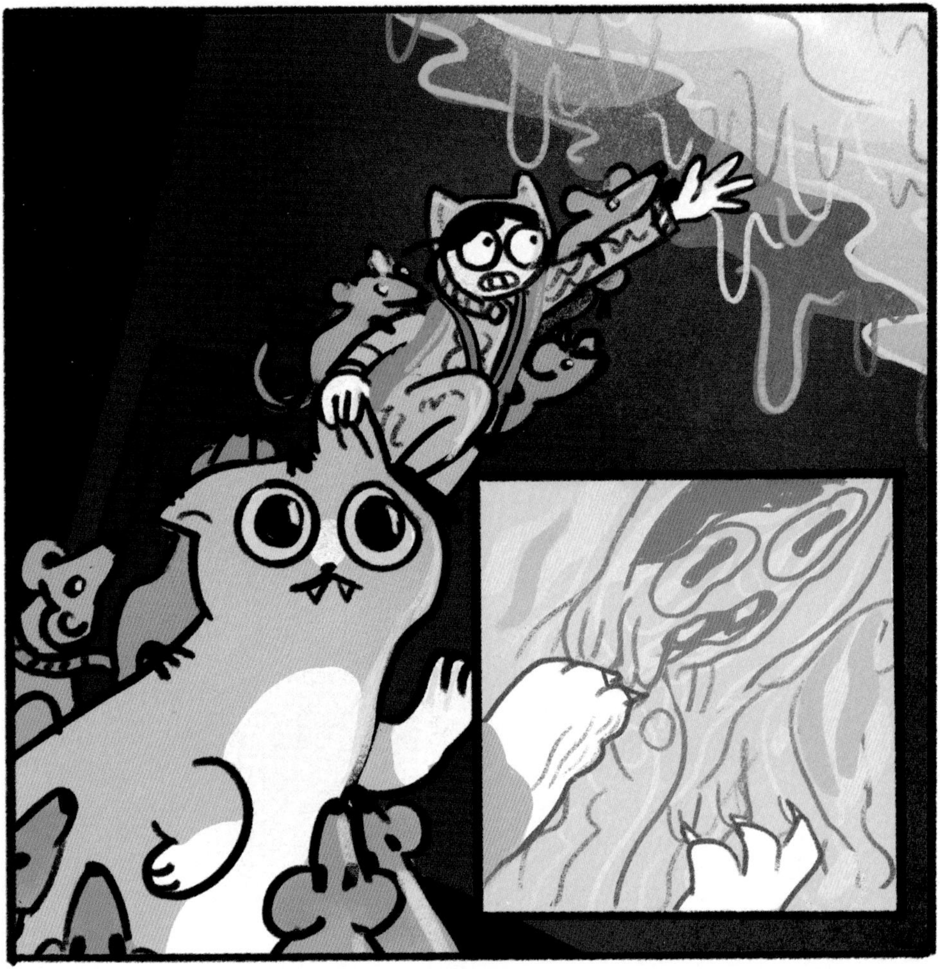

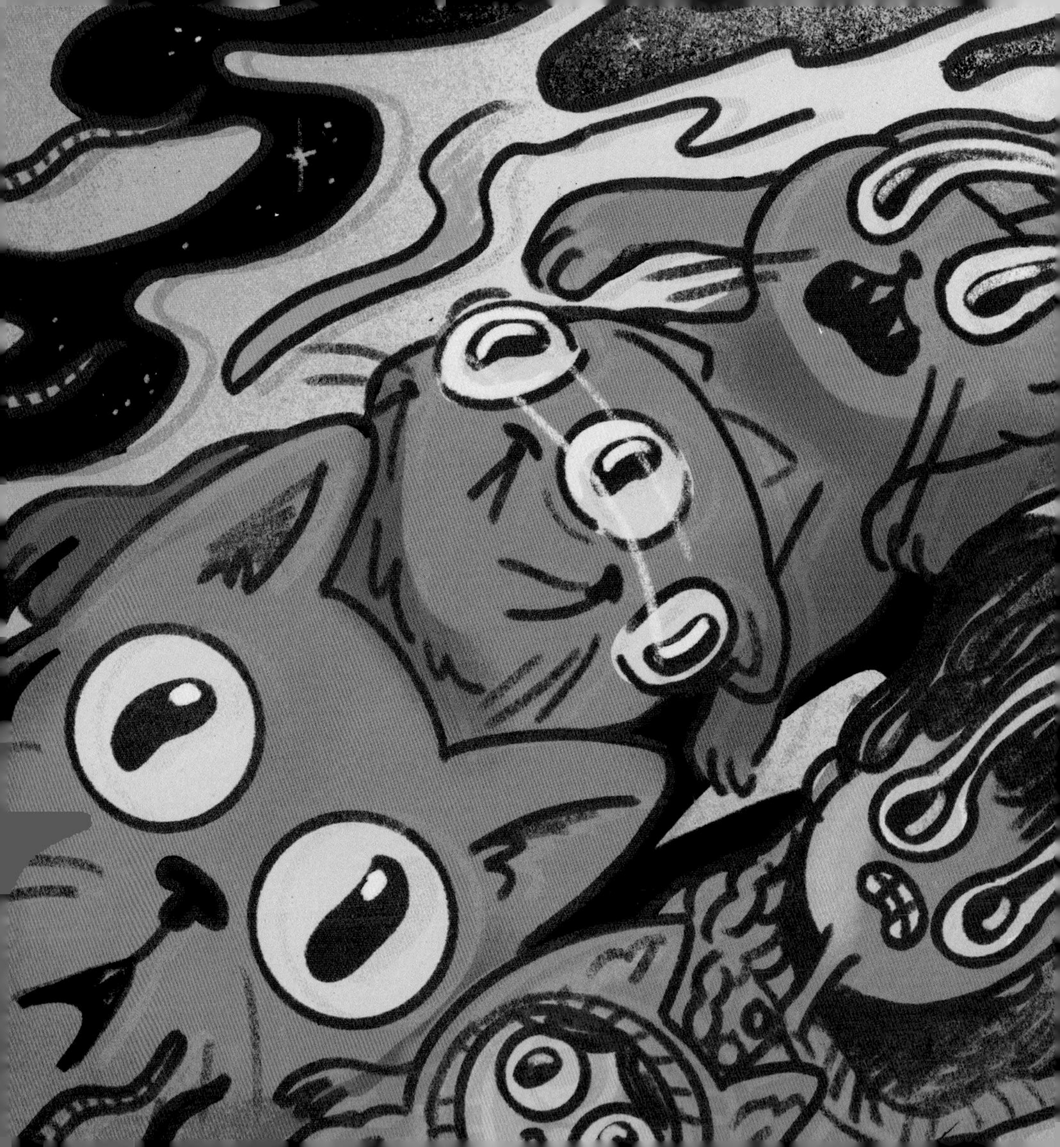

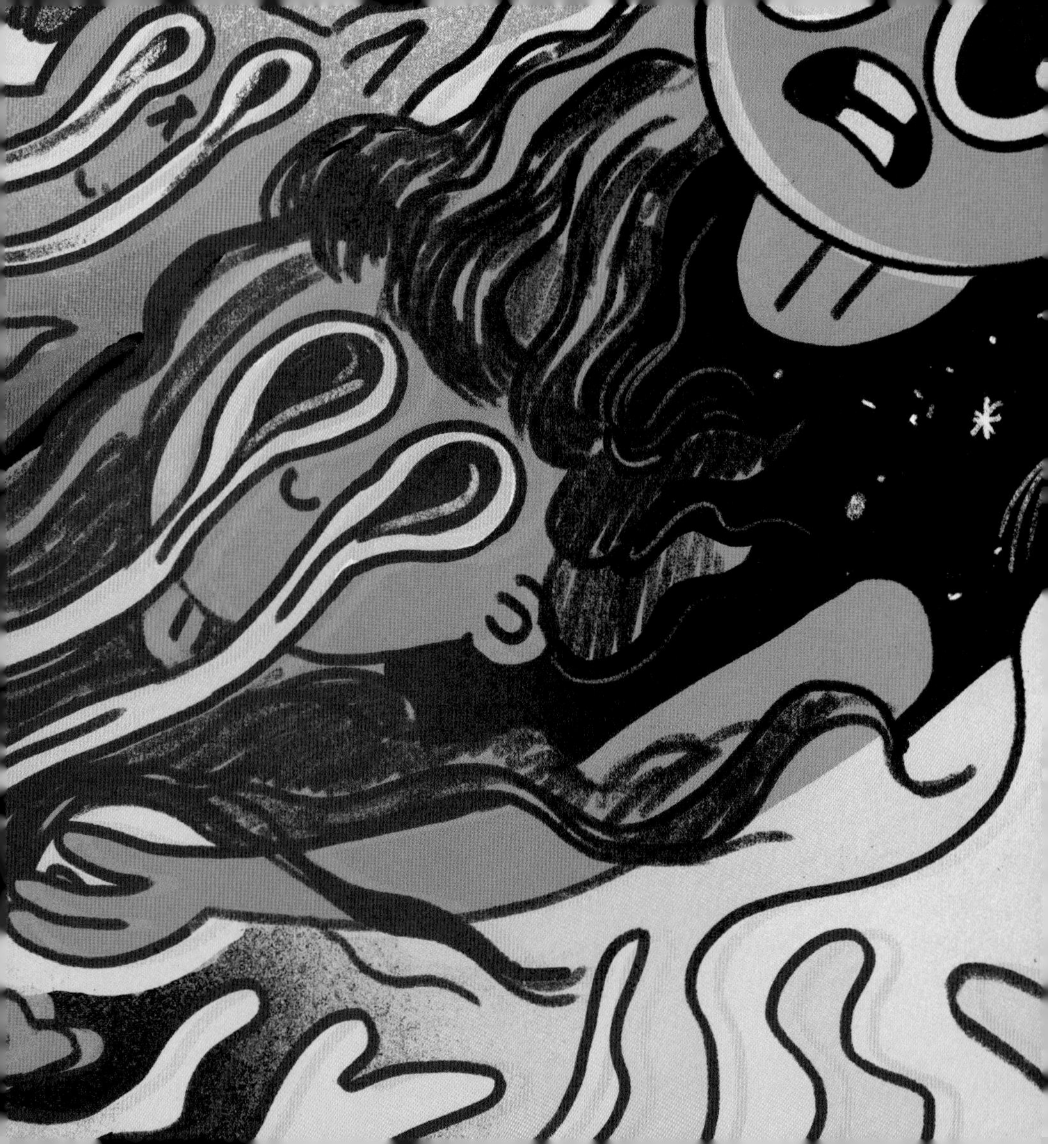

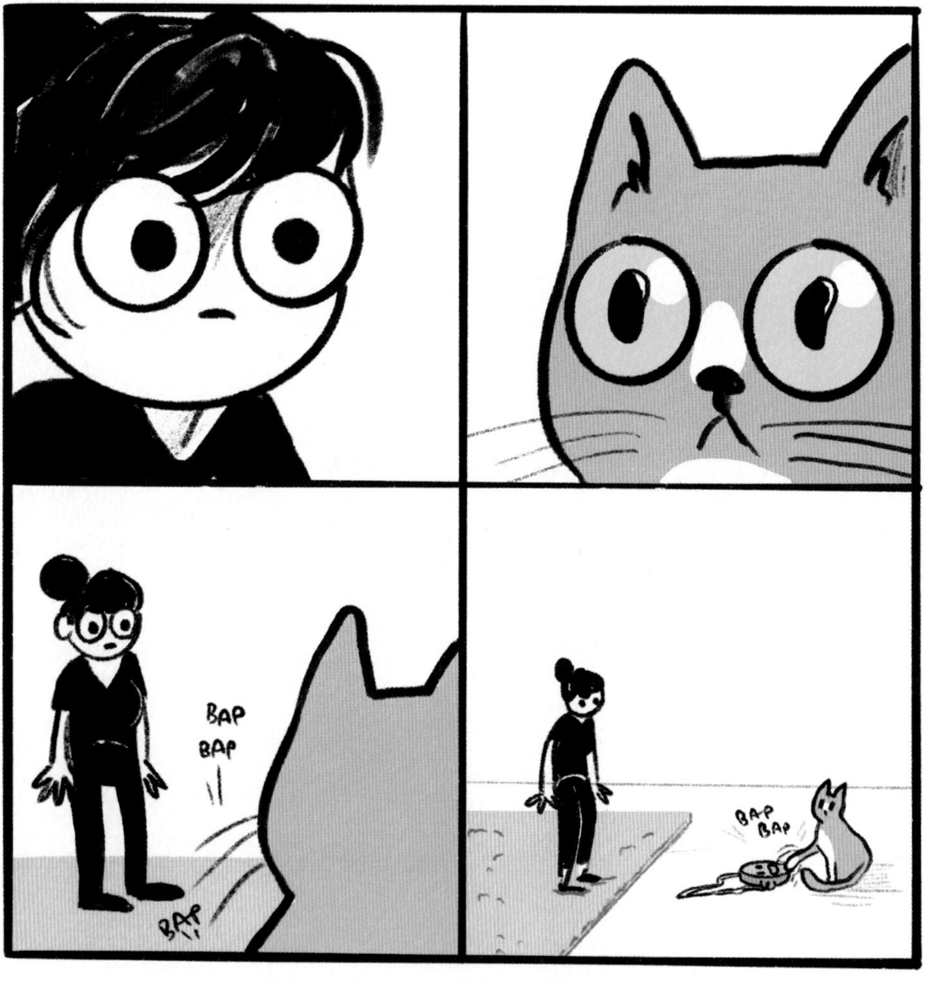
BAP
BAP
BAP
BAP
BAP

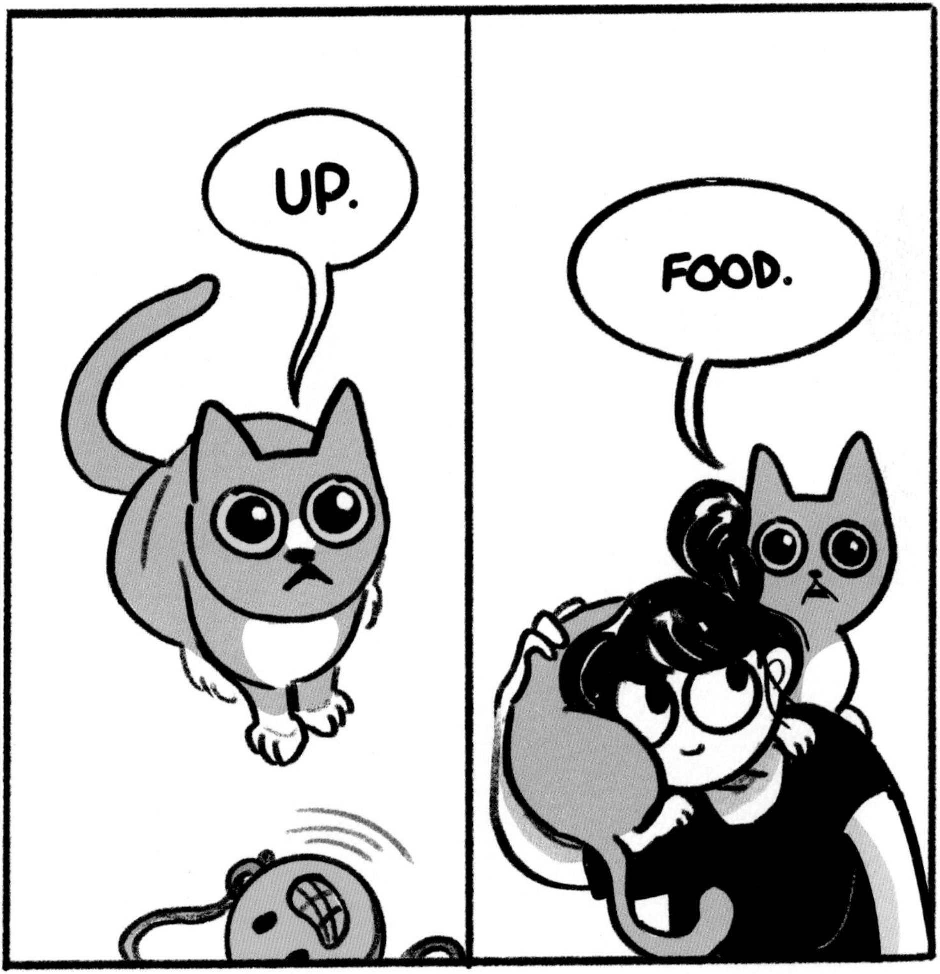
UP.
FOOD.

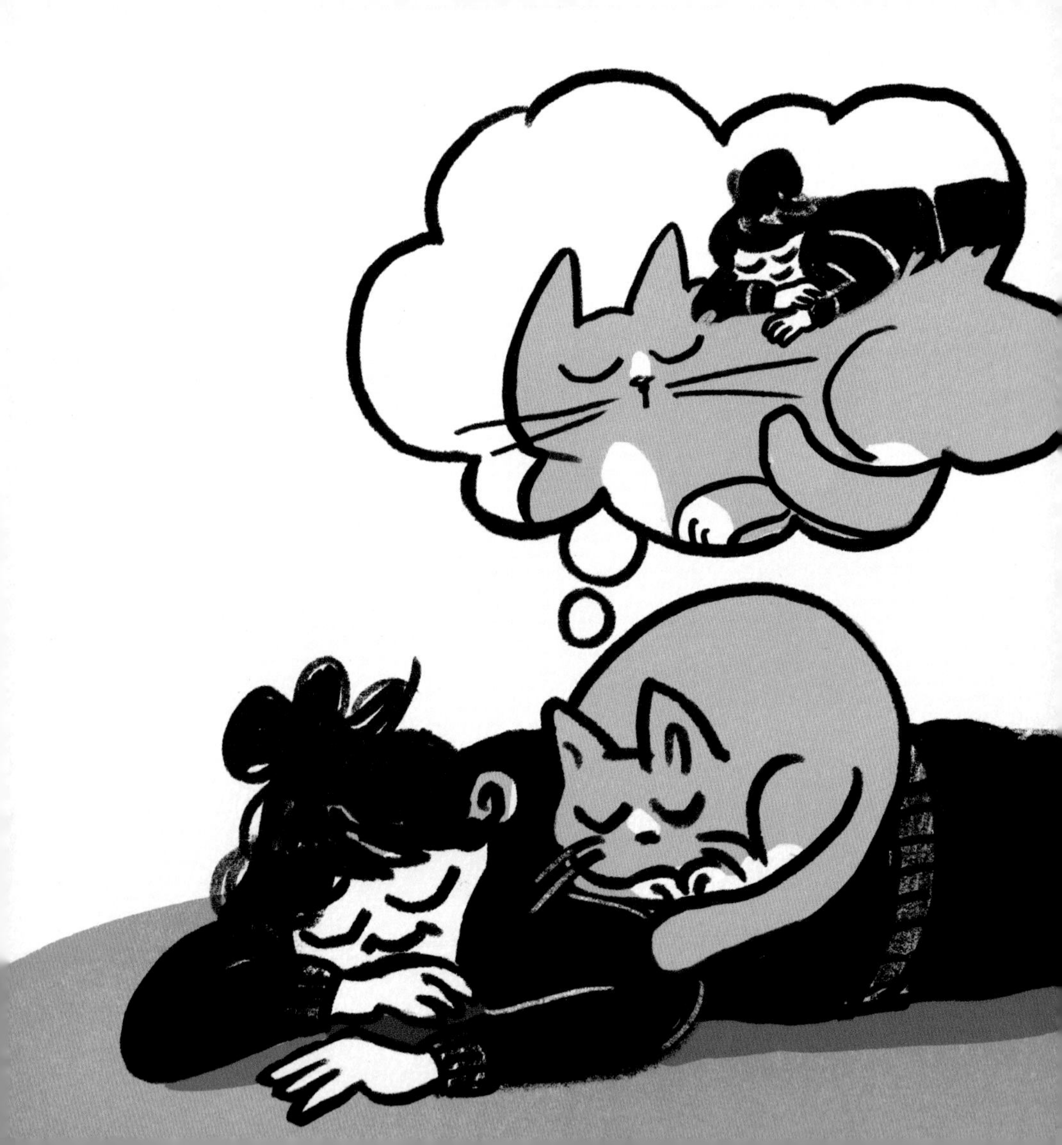

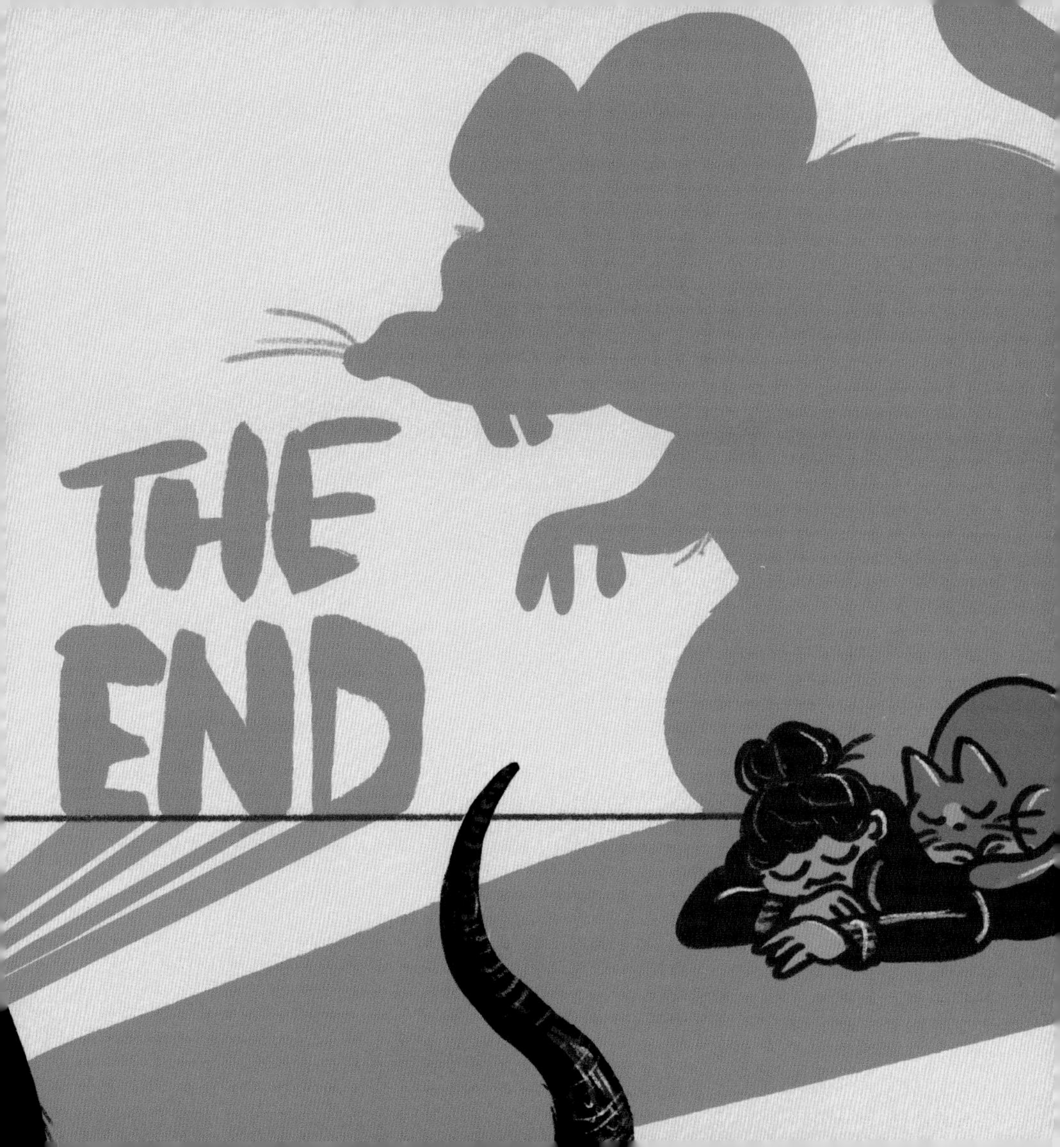
THE END

ACKNOWLEDGMENTS

Thank you to Sean for all the support and belief and for always helping me put things in perspective, figuratively and literally. This book would have no backgrounds without you. To G and J for their patience and love. To Yadira for her trust in me and the excellent care of my children (along with all the other Maestras). To Ashton, without whom none of this could have happened; to Business Hannah, who keeps everything around me afloat; and to la Familia Juarez for their boundless support and flexibility. Thank you to my parents for the homemade sketchbooks and for, along with my grandparents, always enabling my creativity. Thank you to Stu and Annie for being the funniest and best siblings. Thank you to Finn the Boston Terrier (RIP) for bringing my family so much joy. To Griffin, the pro at ironing out plot issues. To Kaveh for the solid advice in response to my panic. To Sarah C for fueling me with laughter. To Sarah Andersen for the advice and direction. To Seth, my wonderful agent, who always pushes me to take my ideas and art to the next level even if it scares me. And of course, thank you to Shannon, my editor. I'm so glad you found me again.

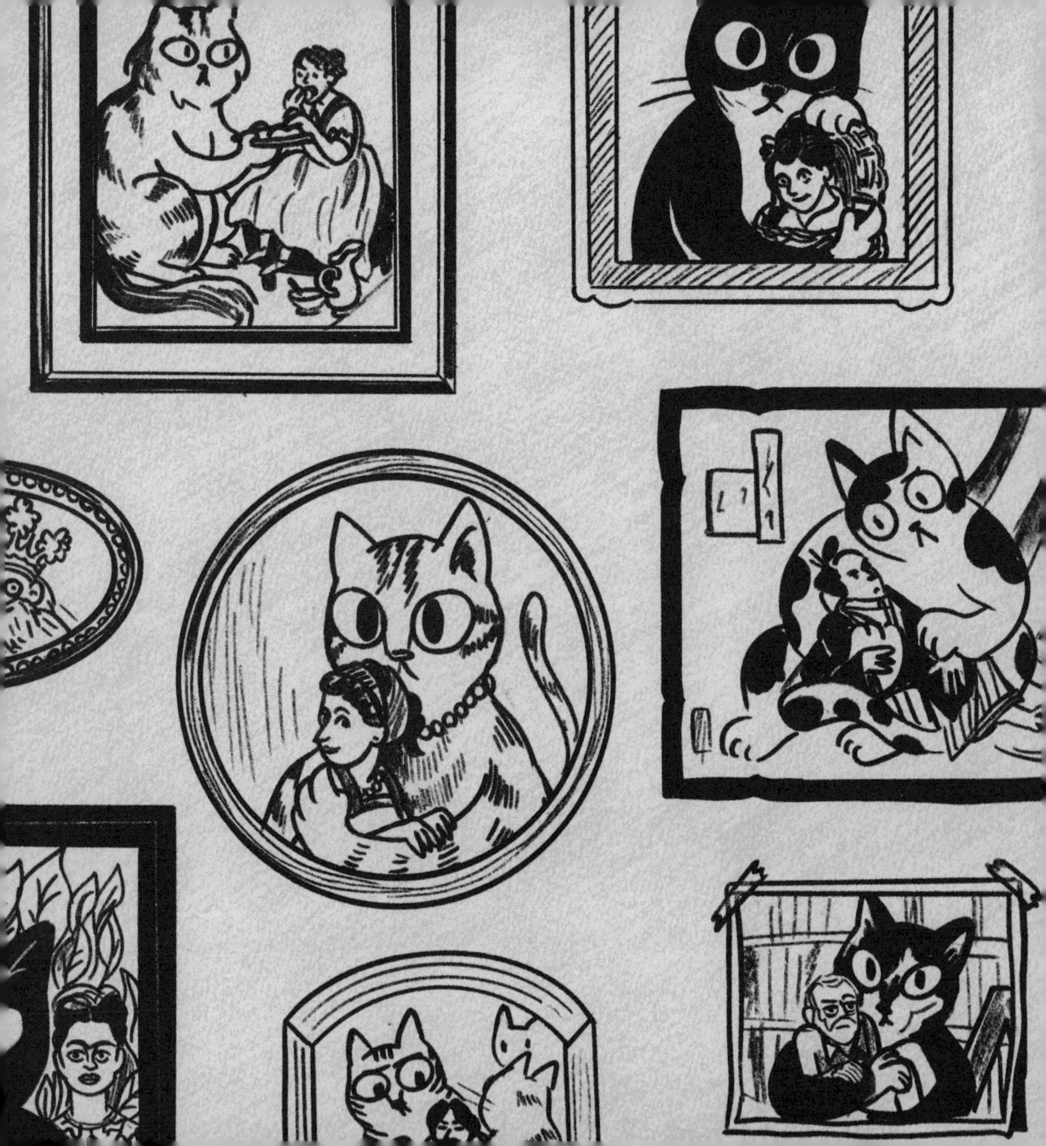